D1034290

PRAYERS
that avail much®
FOR AMERICA

OTHER BOOKS BY GERMAINE COPELAND

NOTABLE BOOKS FROM THE
PRAYERS THAT AVAIL MUCH SERIES

Prayers That Avail Much for the Nations

Prayers That Avail Much

Prayers That Avail Much for Women

Prayers That Avail Much for the Workplace

Prayers That Avail Much for Parents

Prayers That Avail Much for Teens

Prayers That Avail Much for Men

Prayers That Avail Much for Moms

Prayers That Avail Much for Leaders

Prayers That Avail Much for New Believers

Prayers That Avail Much for the College Years

365 Days to a Prayer-Filled Life

A Global Call to Prayer

PRAYERS
that avail much.®
FOR AMERICA

GERMAINE COPELAND

© Copyright 2018– Germaine Copeland

All rights reserved. This book is protected by the copyright laws of the United States of America. This book may not be copied or reprinted for commercial gain or profit. The use of short quotations or occasional page copying for personal or group study is permitted and encouraged. Permission will be granted upon request. Unless otherwise identified, Scripture quotations are taken from The Holy Bible, English Standard Version® (ESV®), copyright © 2001 by Crossway, a publishing ministry of Good News Publishers. Used by permission. All rights reserved. Scripture quotations marked AMP are taken from the Amplified® Bible, Copyright © 2015 by The Lockman Foundation, La Habra, CA 90631. All rights reserved. Used by permission. Scripture quotations marked NKJV are taken from the New King James Version. Copyright © 1982 by Thomas Nelson, Inc. Used by permission. All rights reserved. Scripture quotations marked NLT are taken from the Holy Bible, New Living Translation, copyright 1996, 2004. Used by permission of Tyndale House Publishers. Wheaton, Illinois 60189. All rights reserved. Scripture quotations marked MSG are taken from The Message. Copyright © 1993, 1994, 1995, 1996, 2000, 2001, 2002. Used by permission of NavPress Publishing Group. Scripture quotations marked GW are taken from GOD'S WORD. GOD'S WORD is a copyrighted work of God's Word to the Nations. Quotations are used by permission. Copyright 1995 by God's Word to the Nations. All rights reserved. Scripture quotations marked CEV are taken from the Contemporary English Version Copyright © 1995 by the American Bible Society, New York, NY. All rights reserved. Scripture quotations marked MEV are taken from The Holy Bible, Modern English Version. Copyright © 2014 by Military Bible Association. Published and distributed by Charisma House. All rights reserved. Used by permission. Scripture quotations marked NASB are taken from the NEW AMERICAN STANDARD BIBLE®, Copyright © 1960, 1962, 1963, 1968, 1971, 1972, 1973, 1975 ,1977,

1995 by The Lockman Foundation. Used by permission. Please note that Destiny Image's publishing style capitalizes certain pronouns in Scripture that refer to the Father, Son, and Holy Spirit, and may differ from some publishers' styles.

DESTINY IMAGE® PUBLISHERS, INC.
P.O. Box 310, Shippensburg, PA 17257-0310
"Promoting Inspired Lives."

This book and all other Destiny Image and Destiny Image Fiction books are available at Christian bookstores and distributors worldwide.

Cover design by Eileen Rockwell
Interior design by Terry Clifton

For more information on foreign distributors, call 717-532-3040.
Reach us on the Internet: www.destinyimage.com.

ISBN 13 TP: 978-0-7684-1918-4
ISBN 13 eBook: 978-0-7684-1916-0
ISBN 13 HC: 978-0-7684-1915-3
ISBN 13 LP: 978-0-7684-1917-7

For Worldwide Distribution, Printed in the U.S.A.
1 2 3 4 5 6 7 8 / 22 21 20 19 18

DEDICATION

This book is dedicated to my grandchildren Matthew, Joe, Rachel, Leah, Martha, Christopher, Chandler, Grace, Griffin, Katherine, Luke, and future generations. I pray they will walk with God and help save America for future generations.

ACKNOWLEDGMENTS

This book might not have been written without the encouragement and prayers of others. First, I thank God for the Word Ministries board members who have walked with me and prayed for me for the completion of this book. Also, I am thankful for our pastor, Dr. Jimmy Long, and the church family at Grace Fellowship in Greensboro, Georgia who encouraged me throughout this process.

During the writing of this book my family faced some difficult times, and I am thankful for my friend, Andrell Corbin. She offered expert knowledge and encouragement when I was struggling with my writing. She was my cheerleader and a valiant prayer warrior who interceded for us. Thank you, Andrell.

A special thank you to our son, David, who continues to maintain the business offices for Word Ministries. As always, I thank my husband, Everette, for his love and patience.

CONTENTS

INTRODUCTION

The America I see unfolding today is not the America of my youth. I vividly recall how each morning in our public schools we stood next to our desks and pledged allegiance to our flag. Our teachers read a scripture and we prayed. We honored God and sang: *America, America, God shed His grace on Thee and crown Thy good with brotherhood from sea to shining sea.* We were taught the history of our nation, knew our National Anthem and were thankful that we lived in the land of the free and the home of the brave. During times of war and disasters, citizens came together and prayed for our President, for our military, their families and our nation. During wartime our mothers volunteered at the Red Cross and our fathers who were exempt from war served in their communities. Although, we did not all vote alike, we respected one another and held the same values. We desired freedom, not just for America, but for the world. We believed "wherever the Spirit of the Lord is, there is freedom" (2 Cor. 3:17 NLT).

Somewhere along the way, due to compromise and prayerlessness, the American Church digressed into a powerless position. As a result, reverence for God was exchanged for political correctness and the tolerance of sin. Our nation now reflects the political, economic, and cultural deterioration from that spiritual decline.

But a revolution has begun. Believers are rising up who *agree* that this state of affairs will not be tolerated any longer. Across all denominational, ethnic, and socio-economic lines, believers are banding together to pray in agreement with the Word of God for a spiritual awakening in our land.

I invite you to join me and many others on this prayer adventure. America will rise as we bow our knees before the God and Father of our Lord Jesus Christ, pray and seek His face on behalf of America! "If Americans know who they are, and where they really come from, they will exert themselves even more to surpass previous generations. That is why the study of our history remains of critical importance. Our history is not just the story of who we once were, but of our destiny; not of what we have accomplished, but of our future success."[1] Are you expecting the works of God to be displayed in our nation? Then take your place now in prayer; for it is prayer that will produce the spiritual awakening our nation so desperately needs.

God is moving and America will be saved if God's people who are called by His name will seek first His righteousness and pray in the light of His Word. Jesus said, "I tell you for certain that if you have faith in me, you will do the same things that I am doing. You will do even greater things, now that I am going back to the Father. Ask me, and I will do whatever you ask. This way the Son will bring honor to the Father" (John 14:12-13 CEV).

The day of the "greater things" is here. This compilation of prayers for America is a tool for you to use in praying for divine intervention in our nation. The spiritual awakening is beginning and together, our prayers shall avail much!

Note

1. Larry Schweikart and Michael Allen, *A Patriot's History of the United States: From Columbus's Great Discovery to America's Age of Entitlement* (New York: Sentinel, 2014), 867.

PRAYERS

OF DESTINY

CALLING FOR THE DESTINY AND ASSIGNMENT OF THE UNITED STATES

The time is now to assume our responsibility as the Body of Christ and purpose to obey the Scriptures as it is written:

> *Therefore I exhort first of all that supplications, prayers, intercessions, and giving of thanks be made for all men, for kings and*

all who are in authority, that we may lead a quiet and peaceable life in all godliness and reverence. For this is good and acceptable in the sight of God our Savior, who desires all men to be saved and to come to the knowledge of the truth. For there is one God and one Mediator between God and men, the Man Christ Jesus, who gave Himself a ransom for all, to be testified in due time, for which I was appointed a preacher and an apostle— I am speaking the truth in Christ and not lying—a teacher of the Gentiles in faith and truth (1 Timothy 2:1-7 NKJV).

If ever there was a time for "all God's people to come to the aid of their country," it is now! It is not the time to be downhearted; it is the time to stand up and assume our responsibility! Satan has opposed Jehovah since the beginning, and he has opposed God's purpose and plan for America. Regardless, the Constitution was formed by the founders and "while America did not have a Christian Founding in the sense of creating a theocracy, its Founding was deeply shaped by Christian moral truths.

More important, it created a regime that was hospitable to Christians, but also to practitioners of other religions."[1]

Now is the time to pray!

*"There is no way that Christians, in
a private capacity, can do so much to
promote the work of God and advance
the kingdom of Christ as by prayer."*
—JONATHAN EDWARDS

PRAYERS OF DESTINY

A Personal Commitment to Pray for America

Father, I consecrate myself to You, and expect You to do amazing things here in America. Thank You for leading our founding fathers by the right way that they might find a dwelling place. We thank You for Your goodness and for Your wonderful works to the children of men. Holy Spirit, help me pray in agreement with God's plans and purposes. I trust You to help me pray when I don't know what to pray. I am here to offer supplications, prayers, intercessions and giving of thanks for all men—for kings and for all that are in authority that we may lead a quiet and peaceable life in all godliness and honesty. I thank You for the founders of this nation and reinforce the prayers—prayers that were prayed according to Your will by our founders. Thank You for men who recognized Your providence and created a government to function for Your purposes: to curb evil, to be an instrument in Your hand and to offer freedom of religious expression and the spread of the Gospel.

Lord, You are our judge; Lord, You are our lawgiver; Lord, You are our king, and You will save us. We seek first Your kingdom and Your way of doing and being right with the help of the Holy

Spirit. I, _____, offer this prayer of consecration and commit to pray for America, in the name of Jesus.

SCRIPTURE REFERENCES: *Joshua 3:5; Psalm 107:7-9; 1 Timothy 2:1-2*

Rebuilding the Walls of Salvation for America

O Lord God of heaven, great and awesome God who keeps covenant and steadfast love with those who love You and keep Your commandments, we come before You humbly asking for mercy. Let Your ear be attentive and Your eyes open to hear the prayers of Your children. Holy Spirit, help us stay focused and pray for those who are in places of authority in our government. We confess the sins of the people of America, which we have sinned against You—even I and my father's house have sinned. We have acted very corruptly against You and have not kept the commandment that Jesus commanded us to keep. We allowed moral, social, and political corruption to invade our land. Forgive us and restore Your people to be light and salt in the earth once again. We are Your servants, whom You have redeemed by Your great power and by Your strong hand. O Lord, let Your ear be attentive to the prayer of Your servants who delight to fear Your name. Grant us mercy, O Lord!

Father, we need You! Give us the grace to rebuild the spiritual walls of the United States of America, and send us a spiritual awakening. We desire to have godly social and spiritual reformation in our culture. Give us a vision of restoration and remind us when we are tempted to come down off the wall of freedom that we are doing a great work and we cannot come down.

SCRIPTURE REFERENCES: *Nehemiah 1 and 6:3*

Standing Strong in the Lord Against the Schemes of the Enemy

Again, we come to the throne room that we might find mercy and grace in our nation's time of need. Holy Spirit, put the intercession of Jesus into words we can pray. Clothed in the armor of God, we take our stand against the Luciferian spirit that is attempting to overthrow the plans of our God for America. Today we proclaim our Lord destroys the plans and spoils the schemes of the nations. We are the Body of Christ seated in heavenly places together with Christ Jesus, far above any ruler or authority or power or leader or anything else—not only in this world but also in the world to come. We are seated far above the principalities and powers of secret societies, satanism, Marxism, humanism, Communism, secularism, pedophilia, materialism, greed, and manipulation, declaring the victory of our Lord Jesus Christ who stripped principalities and powers of their power! They tried to kill Him— He arose victorious over death and the grave!

We choose to speak words of life that dispel the darkness! What the Lord has planned will stand forever! His thoughts never change, and our Lord blesses the nation that worships only Him! He blesses His chosen ones, and we are a nation within a nation—the people called by His name to destroy the works of the evil one! Nothing that the leaders of our nation can do—both good and evil—will be hidden from Him. We declare the Lordship of Jesus over the United States of America, and it is in His name that we pray!

SCRIPTURE REFERENCES: *Hebrews 4:16; Ephesians 6:11; Psalm 33; 1 John 3:8*

Prayer of Thanksgiving for America

Father, You are the Creator, the God of heaven, and we thank You for Your steadfast love that endures forever. Our government was appointed by You to fulfill Your purposes and plans on earth even as in heaven. We thank You for our founding fathers who were men of honor and character, who revered You as the Sovereign Creator of heaven and earth. America has been the beacon of liberty. Despite our flaws and shortcomings, we remain a people who believe that "All men are created equal." Thank You that we have freedom to worship You. We thank You that the Gospel is published in our land and we have the freedom to worship You in spirit and in truth. Where the Spirit of the Lord is, there is liberty. Thank You that we are here for such a time as this, in the name of Jesus! Amen.

SCRIPTURE REFERENCES: *Psalm 136:26; Romans 13:1; Matthew 6:10; Genesis 1:26; 2 Corinthians 3:17*

He therefore is the truest friend to the liberty of his country who tries most to promote its virtue, and who, so far as his power and influence extend, will not suffer a man to be chosen into any office of power and trust who is not a wise and virtuous man. ...The sum of all is, if we

would most truly enjoy this gift of Heaven, let us become a virtuous people.

—SAMUEL ADAMS, *founding father and signer of the Declaration of Independence*[2]

If Americans truly want the Republic that their forefathers bled for, they must educate themselves on what the Founding Fathers wanted for America and fight to restore that vision through strict adherence and respect for the Constitution.[3]

Praying for the Fulfillment of America's Vision

Father, in the name of Jesus, thank You for the United States of America that You ordained for Your purposes. We renounce all forms of globalism, freemasonry, and the occult in the name of Jesus and declare the Lordship of Jesus over our nation. We choose to arise and shine for the Light has come and the darkness is exposed. Jesus has been given all authority in heaven and on earth, and He will be with us here in America even until the end of the world. Thank You for calling and anointing men and women to be Your representatives in the land and around the world. Father, we earnestly pray for leaders who will maintain the intent and purposes of our founding fathers and who will uphold the Constitution as it was written so freedom might continue—not the freedom to violate divine laws but the freedom to do what's right. Without a vision this nation will perish. Grant unto Your representatives a boldness to speak truth on behalf of the people. We ask for wise counselors, public servants, military attachés, cultural attachés, and diplomats for every manner of work in our government and around the world. Thank You that our nation is a republic, one nation under God, and that we have more than enough to meet every situation and everything we need to carry out Your great commission. Thank You for hearing our prayer.

Praying for All Government Leaders

Our Father, we pray for godly statesmen/women who are honorable and of good character. Give our government leaders discernment and keep them from being tricked with foolish talk. May they walk as children of the light exposing greed and corruption. Deliver our nation from evil and from those who oppose Your plan for America. Righteousness will guard him whose way is blameless, but wickedness overthrows the sinner. Give our leaders the courage to submit to You and resist being drawn into doing those worthless things that are done in the dark. "There is nothing covered that will not be revealed and hidden that will not be known." Reveal Your will and help them to act with good sense. These are desperate times, and we pray that those You appointed will be strong in You and the power of Your might. Thank You for hearing our prayer! Amen.

SCRIPTURE REFERENCES: *Ephesians 5:6-15 CEV; Proverbs 13:6 NKJV; Matthew 10:26 NKJV*

Praying for God to Be Glorified in America

Our Father in heaven, we honor You for Your name is holy. You made the heavens and the earth and everything in it. You are Lord of heaven and earth! You give life, breath, and everything else to all people. From one person, You made all nations who live on earth, and You decided when and where every nation would be. Thank You, Father, for the United States of America. It is Your desire that all men be saved and come to the knowledge of the truth, and You have formed this nation to proclaim the Gospel so that everyone everywhere will turn to You and repent of their sins. You are never far from any of us, and You give us the power to live, to move, and to be who we are; You satisfy our every need. America is here for the increase of Your kingdom.

The god of this world has come to defy the Most High God, to defeat Your purposes for the United States of America, but we are the Body of Christ strong in the Lord and the power of

Your might! We take our stand, proclaiming the name of the Lord; He is worthy to be praised! Jesus has defeated the hidden powers of darkness, and the gates of hell shall not prevail against the Church. Jesus is building a glorious Church. We release the spirit of salvation to convict and convince the people of sin, righteousness, and judgment. May they turn to You and be saved before the day You have set for the world to be judged with justice by Jesus. You gave proof of this to everyone when You raised Him from the dead. Our hope is in You for another spiritual awakening in our nation that You may be glorified, in the name of Jesus our Lord!

SCRIPTURE REFERENCES: *Acts 17*

Praying for the President to Have a Discerning Heart

In the name of Jesus, we come with a prayer of intercession for the President of the United States. Father, we thank You for the person You have appointed for such a time as this. We ask

You to give Your servant a discerning heart to govern Your people and to distinguish between right and wrong. For who is able to govern this great people of Yours? It's not by might, nor by power, but by Your Spirit. You have shown the people who are called by Your name the power of Your works. You have provided redemption for Your people; You ordained Your covenant forever—holy and awesome is Your name. We pray that our President will fear the Lord, which is the beginning of wisdom. Give him the desire to know and follow Your precepts that he may have good understanding, for to You belongs eternal praise. To God be the glory, great things He has done in the name of His Son, Jesus! Amen!

SCRIPTURE REFERENCES: *Romans 13; 1 Kings 3:9; Zechariah 4:6; Psalm 111*

Praying for the President to Know Wisdom and Instruction

Father, You instructed us to pray for government leaders, and we are here standing in the gap for our President asking You to teach him wisdom's ways and lead him in straight paths. When he walks, he won't be held back; when he runs, he won't stumble. We pray that he will take hold of Your instructions. Holy Spirit, give him the courage to stand on Your promises and never let them go. May he always guard them, for Your words are the key to the life of our nation. We pray that our President will exalt the name of our Lord, and that the God of our salvation will be exalted in America so the whole world will know that You are God. Hold our President safe beyond the reach of the forces of darkness that attempt to hinder him, and save him from violent opponents. For this, O Lord, we will praise You among the nations and sing praises to Your name.

SCRIPTURE REFERENCES: *Romans 13; Proverbs 4:11-13; Psalm 18*

Praying for the President's Cabinet

Father, we ask for the intercession of Jesus as we wait here before You. We not only pray for our President but also for those surrounding him. There is no authority except from God, and the authorities that exist are appointed by God. We pray for men and women who will set aside personal agendas and serve You first, the President, and the American people. We pray for Your kingdom to come and Your will to be done in our nation. Where there is no counsel, the people fall; but in the multitude of counselors there is safety. We thank You for the advisers surrounding our President—the Vice President and the heads of the 15 executive departments. Give them discernment and the understanding to walk uprightly. Give us men and women of understanding who walk uprightly, who have discernment. Without counsel, plans go awry, but in the multitude of counselors they are established. The power of life and death is in the tongue, and we pray these cabinet members will speak words of life for the good of the country and for Your glory!

SCRIPTURE REFERENCES: *Romans 13; Proverbs 11:14; 15:22; 18:21*

Praying for the Military

Father, we put on Your armor and stand against the forces of darkness that are scheming to steal, kill, and destroy the freedom we enjoy as a nation. Thank You for the men and women who lay down their lives for our country.

The conflicts our armed forces are facing are life-and-death situations. Thank You for the military officers and commanders who lean not unto their own understanding but acknowledge You in all their ways. Give them Your wisdom as they lead the men and women under their command, and help them make decisions in conformity with Your will.

Lord, we petition the courts of heaven for a strong military who is ready to defend freedom and those rights You have granted to mankind. We pray they will be instruments of righteousness defeating the plans of the devil while pursuing wholesome relationships with all nations. During a time of conflict, protect our soldiers, and be their constant companion and strength in battle, their refuge in every adversity. We pray for their safe return.

Jesus, thank You for giving Your life so men could be free, and now we pray that we may live to make men free, "while God is marching on."[4] May we all pursue what makes for peace and for mutual upbuilding, in the name of Jesus.

Prayer for the Military and Their Families

Father, we come before You in the mighty name of Your Son, Jesus our Lord. We bear upon our shoulders our Commander-in-Chief and our political and military leaders, praying they will tirelessly seek peaceful settlements to international disputes. Create within the hearts of all men and women a desire for true peace and justice. All things are possible with You.

We plead the blood of Jesus over our troops, and ask You to keep them safe and rescue them from danger. Provide for and protect the families of our armed forces. During times of separation, strengthen them and give them the wisdom to cope with daily challenges in the absence of their loved ones. Thank You for wise counselors who are helping the children of those men and women who are deployed to other nations. May You be their source of comfort and peace that passes understanding.

Father, we are grateful for those who have given their lives for our country. God of all comfort, we ask You to comfort loved ones—wives, children, mothers, fathers, family members, and friends. We call upon Jehovah-Jireh to see to their needs and provide for them according to Your glorious riches.

Father, we are looking forward to that day when there shall be no more war, and the whole earth shall be filled with the knowledge of the glory of the Lord.

Praying for Governors

Holy Spirit, help us pray when we do not know how. First, we ask You to create a desire in the hearts of the citizens of each state to get to know those who are running for the position of governor. Give the voters the wisdom to vote for well-balanced men and women who will acknowledge You in all their ways. Second, we ask You for competent men and women who fear You, for men and women of integrity who hate covetousness and are incorruptible. Father, give governors Your love of justice; may they listen to wise counsel and never follow the advice of the wicked. May they seek Your wisdom in all the responsibilities they bear. May their decisions be according to Your will for the people, in the name of Jesus!

SCRIPTURE REFERENCES: *Exodus 18; Psalm 1*

Praying for the Supreme Court

Our Father who is in heaven, we bring our petition before the throne of grace where we may receive mercy and grace on behalf of our nation. Forgive us for the sin of prayerlessness and have mercy on us according to Your steadfast love and abundant mercy. Blot out our sin and create within us a clean heart and renew a right spirit within us.

Clothed in the armor of God, we take our stand against the anti-Christ spirit that has set himself up as a ruling spirit in the halls of our Supreme Court and in the lower courts. We submit to You, the Lord God Almighty, the Most High who is the first cause of everything, and we resist the devil. The resurrection power of our Lord has stripped Satan of his power! Hallelujah! In the name of Jesus, we stand here declaring the lordship of Jesus over our Supreme Court and the lower courts. Father, remove any man or woman who rules contrary to Your will, and we ask for justices who will use Your Word as their primary source for direction as they carry out their duties before You. May the faith of those who believe in the Bible never fail, and we pray they will strengthen one another. We release a spirit of salvation to any Supreme Court justice who is unsaved.

We pray that they all shall remember the Lord our God that You may establish Your covenant in our nation. May these men and women rule in the fear of God, and we pray their decisions will be according to Your will and for Your glory. "May they hate evil, and love good, and establish justice in the name of Jesus" (Amos 5:14 ESV).

Praying for the Senate and House of Representatives

Almighty God, You are the just Judge and the righteous Lawgiver. We are here to build up the wall and stand in the breach before You for our nation. Today, we unite in prayer for our legislative branch of government—the United States Congress and our senators and representatives.

We pray that they will be men and women who believe in the absolute truth of Your Word, who have not bowed down to secular humanism, contemporary customs, and culture. Give us leaders who believe in the Ten Commandments, the Declaration of Independence, and the Constitution of these United States of America and its Bill of Rights. We ask You for senators and representatives who are wise and understanding and by their good conduct they will show their works in the meekness of wisdom. May they be free from bitter jealousy and selfish ambition, for where jealousy and selfish ambition exist there is disorder and vile practice. Give them wisdom that comes down from above, which is peaceable, gentle, open to reason, full of mercy and good fruits, impartial, and sincere. May we as Your people vote for men and women of integrity who will uphold the Constitution, always ethical and fair in their deliberations and judgments. When temptations arise, reveal the way of escape and give our senators and representatives the strength to stand for truth and righteousness and pass laws that will honor You. Father, give them discernment to walk in paths of righteousness, revering Your name. We pray that those who oppose Your will for our nation will come to the knowledge of the truth and choose to carry out Your plans for our nation, in the name of Jesus.

Appoint judges and officials for yourselves from each of your tribes in all the towns the Lord your God is giving you. They must judge the people fairly. You must never twist justice or show partiality. Never accept a bribe, for bribes blind the eyes of the wise and corrupt the decisions of the godly. Let true justice prevail, so you may live and occupy the land that the Lord your God is giving you (Deuteronomy 16:18-20 NLT).

Praying for the Judges of Our Land

Father, we pray for judges who will protect the sanctity of innocent life from conception to natural birth. We thank You for the gift of our nation and acknowledge that You alone rule the world with justice. You have placed in the hands of men and women the solemn duty of participating in the shaping of our government. We ask You for government leaders and judges who take life seriously. We ask You to give them insight and discernment in their deliberations. You have entrusted government leaders with the responsibility of nominating men and women as judges in our court system. May our high court make wise decisions in the many cases they hear. "The heart of the wise makes his speech judicious and adds persuasiveness to his lips."

SCRIPTURE REFERENCE: *Proverbs 16:23*

Praying for American Citizens

Father, in the name of Jesus, we pray for the people of this great nation. As we pray, we choose to forgive those who have turned their backs on our God and our history. Lead them by Your Spirit to repentance by Your goodness. It is our prayer that Your Word will run swiftly throughout every city and village of this country. Holy Spirit, we thank You for giving our government officials a spirit of counsel and wisdom so that they may communicate a message of hope for this country. You give the wise answers, and we pray that their words will be a demonstration of Your wisdom operating in them. In the name of Jesus, we pull down the stronghold of deception working to entrap the people. Father, watch over everyone who shows good sense, and frustrate the plans of deceitful liars. We decree and declare that truth shall prevail! Prepare the hearts of the citizens to hear words that will persuade them that Your will must be done in our nation and then we will fulfill our destiny. We pray that in a time of trouble men's hearts will not fail them, but they will continue in faith. We pray that You will give us, the citizens of heaven and America, the discerning of the signs of the times. Give the people of this nation a spirit of wisdom and revelation in the knowledge of You. May our prayers for this nation release rivers of living water for the healing of America in the name of Jesus. Amen.

Praying in Agreement with Prayers from Past

O Lord our Heavenly Father, high and mighty King of kings, and Lord of lords, who dost from thy throne behold all the dwellers on earth and reignest with power supreme and uncontrolled over all the Kingdoms, Empires and Governments; look down in mercy, we beseech Thee, on these our American States, who have fled to Thee from the rod of the oppressor and thrown themselves on Thy gracious protection, desiring to be henceforth dependent only on Thee. To Thee have they appealed for the righteousness of their cause; to Thee do they now look up for that countenance and support, which Thou alone canst give. Take them, therefore, Heavenly Father, under Thy nurturing care; give them wisdom in Council and valor in the field; defeat the malicious designs of our cruel adversaries; convince them of the unrighteousness of their Cause and if they persist in their sanguinary purposes, of own unerring justice, sounding in their hearts, constrain them to drop the weapons of war from their unnerved hands in the day of battle!

Be Thou present, O God of wisdom, and direct the councils of this honorable assembly; enable them to settle things on the best and surest foundation. That the scene of blood may be speedily closed; that order, harmony and peace may be effectually restored, and truth and justice, religion and piety, prevail and flourish amongst the people. Preserve the health of their bodies and vigor of their minds; shower down on them and the millions they here represent, such temporal blessings as Thou seest expedient for them in this world and crown them with everlasting glory in the world to come. All this we ask in the name and through the merits of Jesus Christ, Thy Son and our Savior. Amen.

—The Prayer in the First Congress, *1774 was led by Dr. Jacob Duche, Rector of Christ Church, Philadelphia,* Pennsylvania[5]

For we must consider that we shall be as a city upon a hill. The eyes of all people are upon us.
—JOHN WINTHROP, *"A Model of Christian Charity," 1630*

No greater thing could come to our land today than revival of the spirit of faith—a revival that would sweep through the homes of the nation and stir the hearts of men and women of all faiths to a reassertion of their belief in God and their dedication to His will for themselves and for their world. I doubt if there is any problem—social, political or economic— that would not melt away before the fires of such spiritual revival.
—FRANKLIN DELANO ROOSEVELT[6]

The Americans combine the notions of Christianity and of liberty so intimately in their

minds, that it is impossible to make them con-
ceive the one without the other.... [They have]
an ostensible respect for Christian morality
and virtue...[and] almost all education is
entrusted to the clergy.

—ALEXIS DE TOCQUEVILLE,
Democracy in America

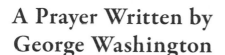

A Prayer Written by George Washington

I now make it my earnest prayer, that God
would have you, and the State over which you
preside, in his holy protection; that he would
incline the hearts of the citizens to cultivate
a spirit of subordination and obedience to
Government; to entertain a brotherly affec-
tion and love for one another, for their fellow
citizens of the United States at large; and, par-
ticularly, for their brethren who have served
in the Geld; and finally, that he would most

graciously be pleased to dispose us all to do justice, to love mercy, and to demean ourselves with that charity, humility, and [peaceful] temper of the mind, which were the characteristics of the divine Author of our blessed religion; without an humble imitation of whose example, in these things, we can never hope to be a happy Nation.

—Closing prayer from a letter sent to the thirteen governors and state legislators upon his resignation as Commander-in-Chief

In regard to this Great Book, I have but to say it is the best gift God has given to man. All the good the Savior gave to the world was communicated through this book.

—ABRAHAM LINCOLN

All of us who were engaged in the struggle must have observed frequent instances of

superintending providence in our favor. To that kind providence we owe this happy opportunity of consulting in peace on the means of establishing our future national felicity. And have we now forgotten that powerful friend? Or do we imagine that we no longer need his assistance? I have lived, Sir, a long time, and the longer I live, the more convincing proofs I see of this truth—that God governs in the affairs of men. And if a sparrow cannot fall to the Ground without his Notice, is it probable that an Empire can rise without his Aid?

—BENJAMIN FRANKLIN, *to colleagues at the Constitutional Convention*

But what do we mean by the American Revolution? Do we mean the American war? The Revolution was effected before the war commenced. The Revolution was in the minds and hearts of the people; a change in their religious sentiments, of their duties and obligations...

This radical change in the principles, opinions, sentiments, and affections of the people was the real American Revolution.

—JOHN ADAMS, *letter to H. Niles, February 13, 1818*

Among the features peculiar to the political system of the United States, is the perfect equality of rights which it secures to every religious sect.

—JAMES MADISON, *letter to Jacob de la Motta, August 1820*

Notes

1. Mark David Hall, "Did America Have a Christian Founding?" The Heritage Foundation, June 7, 2011, http://www.heritage.org/political-process/report/did-america-have-christian-founding.

2. Samuel Adams, qtd. in William Vincent Wells, *The Life and Public Service of Samuel Adams,* Volume 1 (1865).

3. Richardinman, "What Did the Founding Fathers Want for America?" Our Turning Point, March 17, 2012, The Proper Role of Government, http://www.ourtp.org/blogs/blog/our-turning-point/personal-responsibility/2012/03/17/what-did-the-founding-fathers-want-for-america.

4. "Battle Hymn of the Republic" by Julia Ward Howe, public domain.

5. "First Prayer of the Continental Congress," The Office of the Chaplain United States House of Representatives, accessed December 24, 2017, https://chaplain.house.gov/archive/continental.html.

6. Franklin D. Roosevelt, "Radio Address on Brotherhood Day," in *Public Papers of the Presidents of the United States: F.D. Roosevelt, 1936* vol. 5, 86.

PRAYERS
OF PROMISE

A PROMISE FROM THE OLD TESTAMENT

In the Old Testament it is written: "If My people who are called by My name will humble themselves, and pray and seek My face, and turn from their wicked ways, then I will hear from heaven, and will forgive their sin and heal their land" (2 Chron. 7:14 NKJV). The prayers of the righteous, those who are called by the name of our God, will avail much if we meet the conditions. It is time to arise from our slumber and follow the instructions. Let us meet the conditions by humbling ourselves, praying and seeking the face of our God, and turning from our wicked ways.

PRAYERS OF PROMISE

Personal Prayer of Humility

Father, I desire to meet the conditions of Second Chronicles 7:14. I am here to humble myself before You. Search me, O God, and know my heart; try me, and know my concerns, and see if there is any rebellious way in me, and lead me in the ancient way (see Ps. 139:23-24). O God, save me by Your name, and judge me by Your strength (see Ps. 54:1). I repent for not keeping the commandment that Jesus gave to His followers. I confess that I was more concerned for myself than my brothers and sisters. Too often I demanded to have it my way. Forgive me, merciful Father. Not my will, but Yours be done. I submit myself to the elders. I submit myself before my brothers and sisters and clothe myself with humility, because You resist the proud but You give grace to the humble. I am myself under Your mighty hand and cast all my care upon You because You care for me. It is by the gift of grace that I am sober and watchful. The adversary is walking around as a roaring lion, seeking whom he may devour. He is here attempting to swallow up America through deception. I resist him firmly in the faith (see 1 Pet. 5:5-9). Your plan and purpose for America shall be completed in the mighty, majestic name of Jesus Christ of Nazareth! Amen.

Leave your country, your family, and your relatives and go to the land that I will show you. I will bless you and make your descendants into a great nation. You will become famous and be a blessing to others. I will bless anyone who blesses you, but I will put a curse on anyone who puts a curse on you. Everyone on earth will be blessed because of you (Genesis 12:1-3 CEV).

Praying for the Peace of Jerusalem

Father, thank You for establishing America and giving us government leaders who continue to bless Israel. Jerusalem is forever, and we thank You that America is a nation that blesses Israel and we are blessed. We pray for the peace of Jerusalem, and thank You that America stands with her and is a friend that sticks closer than a brother. Thank You for prospering the nations who love the Holy City. We pray that peace may be within her walls and prosperity within her palaces. We ask of You and You tell us remarkable secrets we do not know about things to come. Thank You for fulfilling Your promise to heal Jerusalem's wounds and give her prosperity and true peace. You promised to cleanse Israel of their sins against You and forgive all her sins of rebellion. This city will bring You joy, glory, and honor before all the nations of the earth! The people of the world will see all the good You do for Your people and tremble with awe at the peace and prosperity You provide for them. Jesus has made peace between Jews and Gentiles, and He has united us by breaking down the wall of hatred that separated us. He has brought Jews and Gentiles together as though we were only one person. As always we offer this in the name of Your Son and our Savior, Jesus Christ of Nazareth.

SCRIPTURE REFERENCES: *Psalm 122:5-7; Jeremiah 33:3, 6-9; Ephesians 2:14-16*

Praying the Lord's Prayer for our Nation

Our Father in heaven, we bless Your Holy name. We magnify the name above all names, Jesus. You are the Almighty God of blessings, the God of might and strength. You are our peace, the hope of salvation for our nation. You are the Highest Sovereign of the heavens and the earth. Hallowed be Your name! May Your kingdom come and Your will be done in our nation. We pray that You will create Your desires within the hearts of Your people. May Your Word run swiftly throughout the streets of our cities, and we pray for Your will to prevail in the halls of Congress. Holy Spirit, teach us to seek first the kingdom of God and His ways.

Give us ministers who will proclaim the Gospel and teach the Scriptures with great care, passion, and conviction. I pray that once again we will hunger and thirst for righteousness and do Your will. Give us our daily bread as we turn to Jesus, who is the Bread of Life. Today, we desire spiritual manna that teaches us how to lay aside the bread of bitterness, anger, rage, gossip, discontent, and self-pity. We pray for the restoration of the family unit as You intended. Help husbands and wives speak grace-filled words to one another and to their children. The Bread of Life is our peace, and we pray that there will be peace in our nation. We pray for government leaders who will receive the Bread of Life as wisdom in all their decisions.

Father, as I sit here meditating on Your will and plan for my life and America, I choose to be kind, compassionate, and forgive others in the same way God forgave me in Christ. Lord, lead us not into temptation. Come and heal our land. We are a broken, divided nation and we need guidance and protection against sin and the forces of darkness. With every temptation, You provide a way of escape. Thank You, Jesus, for giving Yourself for our sins that You might deliver us from this present evil world according to the will of God. To God be the glory for ever and ever. Your kingdom come, Your will be done in our nation even as it is in heaven.

SCRIPTURE REFERENCES: *Matthew 6:9-13; Ephesians 5*

Awake Church! Awake America!

Father, You have told us to be "strong in the Lord and the power of His might" (Eph. 6:10 NKJV). You have called us to bless Israel and preach repentance for the kingdom of heaven is at hand. We are here to acknowledge You, the Most High God, and take our stand against the spiritual wickedness in high places, in the name of Jesus. Reveal the hearts of those in leadership positions and expose any secret agenda that is contrary to Your Word and will in their everyday decisions. Disappoint the devices of the crafty that their hands may not form their enterprise (see Job 5:12). We take authority over all lying and deceiving spirits that desire to ascend the throne of this nation. May the principalities and powers that have endeavored to overtake this nation be restrained. Cause them to cease and desist in their maneuvers against us. Keep deception and lies from us according to Proverbs 30:8-10. O God, we pour out our hearts for America that You will have mercy on this nation and heal our land. Touch the hearts and minds of all people, leadership in particular, that they will pursue righteousness and justice and that Your name will be glorified. Let no one hijack Your agenda from our hearts or deceive us into their plans. Rather, open our eyes and ears and give us the ability to discern Your Word and will for our nation, including the times and seasons that Your purpose may be wrought in us and that men everywhere would be granted grace and space to repent and turn to You. Dear Father God, we ask You to grant these and other blessings, and we thank You in advance for them in the matchless, imperial name of our Lord and Savior Jesus Christ.[1] Amen!

As believers we are to look at those things which are eternal. God works through Kingdom-minded people who are salt and light in our nation, helping to create a quiet atmosphere where we can go about our business of living simply, in humble contemplation rather than unrest, chaos, and fear. The enemy of our souls infiltrated and has attempted to control our thinking so we will fit into a culture that seeks to eliminate God from our society.

There is no leveler like Christianity, but it levels by lifting all who receive it to the lofty table-land of a true character and of undying hope both for this world and the next.

—JONATHAN EDWARDS

Praying for the American Church

Father, cleanse us from dead works and old wineskins. In the name of Jesus we break and destroy every wall of tradition that has trapped us in lifeless worship and empty rituals. We stand against false teachings that promote and bring division in the Church of Jesus Christ. Father, give us ministers who teach the uncompromised Word of God. Thank You for this mighty move of Your Spirit upon the earth today! We pray for youth pastors who will encourage the youth to develop a spirit of excellence. May they be men and women of godly character who will be Kingdom builders. We pray that the Church of Jesus Christ will walk in love and the power of the Holy Spirit. Even though we are different denominations and have different points of doctrine, may we be the Church saturated by prayer and passionate worship. May we be the church exploding in waves of revival, bringing life to lifeless congregations, and we ask You to ignite the youngest believers to do exploits to the glory of the Father, in the name of Jesus!

SCRIPTURE REFERENCES: *Ephesians 4*

Praying for The Media

Father, it is written that righteousness exalts a nation, but sin is a disgrace to any people. We ask You to provide the media outlets—television, radio, magazines, newspapers—with staff members and executives who are committed to truth and integrity. In the name of Jesus we stand against the prince of the power of the air and all the powers of deception. We pray that the atmosphere will be charged with truth. Justice will no longer be driven back and righteousness will no longer stand at a distance; truth shall be spoken, in the name of Jesus.

SCRIPTURE REFERENCES: *Proverbs 14:34; Ephesians 6:10-12; 4:15; Proverbs 3:1-4; Isaiah 59:14*

If America is to survive we must elect more God-centered men and women to public office.
BILLY GRAHAM

Praying for the Government

First of all, we offer supplications, prayers, intercessions, and thanksgiving for everyone—for our President and all who are in authority—that we may lead a quiet and peaceful life in all godliness and honesty. Father, the eternal purpose is to give all men the opportunity to be saved and to come to the knowledge of the truth. Give us leaders who want to prepare our nation for the advancement of the kingdom of God—men and women who will be faithful and pursue righteousness and justice with boldness. Give us governmental authorities who assume their offices with clean hands and pure hearts. We ask You to give them knowledge and discretion. May their decisions show integrity, seriousness, and soundness of speech that cannot be condemned. We pray they will manage as King David did, with integrity of heart and with skillful hands as they lead the people of this great nation, in the name of Jesus.

SCRIPTURE REFERENCES: *1 Timothy 2:1-4*

Praying for the Educational System

Father, forgive us for allowing our education systems to be infiltrated with false, unsound doctrines and untruths. All wisdom and truth come from You and You alone. We pray for the Secretary of Education, professors, college presidents, teachers, principals, school counselors, and all those who run these systems from preschool to post-graduate work. Draw these educators back to You, and teach them the fear of the Lord is the beginning of wisdom. You made light to shine in the darkness, and we ask You to shine the light of the knowledge of Your glory from classroom to classroom, from college dorms to the academics. God, we pray that You will move by Your spirit into our schools and universities so that they become open to Jesus and the wisdom and knowledge hidden *for* us *in* Him. Father, I ask You to show us how and give us the grace to bring Your Word back to a place of prominence in our education, churches, and families. I ask all of this in the name of Jesus in accordance with Your Word.

Praying for the Economy

Our Father in heaven, we bless Your holy name. Your kingdom come; Your will be done on earth as it is in heaven. In Jesus' name we call for powerful leaders who will speak truly, live truly, and deal truly; who will walk in integrity in trade and commerce. Thank You for giving them the desire to study and obtain the education necessary for these positions. We pray they will recognize You in all their deliberations and ask You for wisdom that only You can give. We pray they will make judgments in their gates that are for truth, justice, and peace. May they be a people who lean not unto their own understanding, but in all their ways they will learn to acknowledge You, and You shall direct their paths. Give them creative ideas as they promote the proper flow and balance of the production of resources, the distribution of resources, and the consumption of resources. We ask You to give us unpresumptuous economic leaders who trust in the living God, who ask for and receive wisdom and understanding. Father, thank You for appointing and anointing leaders who live under the banner of the Lord's provision. Today, we lift up Wall Street, the bankers, and the economists, praying they will do according to all that You have commanded us. It is our prayer that these leaders will be governed by the law of love, giving tithes and offerings, and they will feed the hungry and give them something to drink; they will welcome strangers, shelter and clothe them, provide help for the sick and infirmed, and minister to those in prison in the name of Jesus.

SCRIPTURE REFERENCES: *Matthew 6:9-10; Ephesians 4:15, Proverbs 3:5-6; Zechariah 8:16 18; Matthew 25:35*

Praying for the Entertainment Industry

Father, we honor You today as the God of creation and we worship Your majesty. Forgive us, Your people who are called by Your name, for neglecting to pray for the field of entertainment here in America. Today, we ask You to give us the wisdom and show us how to pray for our brothers and sisters who work as Your ministers in the arts, entertainment, and sports. You have called them to go out into the world uncorrupted, a breath of fresh air in this squalid and polluted society. Father, we pray they will carry the light-giving Message into the night and provide people with a glimpse of good living and of You, the living God. (Philippians 2:14-16 MSG)

We lift up the writers, producers, graphic artists, photographers, cartoonists, designers, and artisans praying they will be filled with Your spirit. We ask You to give them wisdom and make them skilled craftsmen/women in all they do. Thank You for giving them all kinds of artistic skills, including the ability to design with ideas that flow from Your throne. (Exodus 36:30 CEV)

Together with our brothers and sisters we take a stand against the forces of darkness that attempt to silence a moral voice in the field of entertainment, arts and sports. The gates of hell will not prevail against the Kingdom of God in our nation. We put on the whole armor of God and we stand strong in the Lord and the power of His might against the perverse spirit seeking to control music that is influencing our youth to do down paths of self-destruction. In the name of Jesus, we say, "Let there be light!" The awesome presence of God will be like thunder and lightning revealing new songs that create a hunger in the hearts and minds of our youth to know the LORD. We ask You to release glory and shatter the darkness! We pray that Your light will infuse the spirits of the people with revelation of who You are. Give them songs that will be majestic anthems of praise and express Kingdom authority! Jesus is Lord!

Holy Spirit, perfect the fruit of our lips as we praise You for giving Your witnesses the necessary skills to excel in sports! We thank You for a spiritual awakening in the field of sports. Give Christian athletes increased opportunities to share the Good News of the Gospel with boldness. May they be examples of integrity and right living. We ask for coaches who serve You and are not ashamed to live a holy life before the eyes of society.

Our hearts cry out for fashion designers who will promote modesty and good character. Give them ideas for clothing with a kingdom-inspired message. Open doors of favor and make crooked places straight so they can move into their destiny. May their designs speak life, in the name of Jesus.

Father, send a spiritual revolution in the arts. Give us filmmakers, artists, directors, actors, and those who work with them a heart like Yours. We proclaim that the enemy of light will be pushed back as television shows, movies, and plays are released that have a moral base and celebrate positive relationships. Father, thank You for guardian angels You have assigned to protect child performers. We ask You to surround them with people of integrity who desire the best for them. May Christian painters, sculptors, architects, and decorators release works inspired by the Holy Spirit, like the cathedrals of old point the viewers toward God and creation.

With our hands lifted up we stand praying for an explosion of supernatural creativity that will challenge our world to think once more that You are God and there is none beside You for the earth is Yours and the fullness thereof. In the name of Jesus, let Your Kingdom come and Your will be done on earth even as it is in heaven!

(Based on "Celebration" prayer from *Prayers That Avail Much for Leaders* by Germaine Copeland and Lane Holland)

SCRIPTURE REFERENCES: *Exodus 31:3; Proverbs 18:15-16 MSG; 2 Corinthians 4:1-6*

Praying for the Family

Father, we come to You with broken hearts, crying out for the families of our nation. Satan has launched an assault against the family through social media, education, and our justice system. We have read that in the beginning when You made man in Your image, You made them male and female. For this reason, a man shall leave his father and mother, be joined to his wife, and the two shall become one flesh. In the name of Jesus, we choose to forgive those who have turned away from Your plan and purposes for the family unit. Holy Spirit, convict and convince them of sin, righteousness, and judgment.

We bow our knees to You, the Father of our Lord Jesus Christ, from whom the whole family in heaven and earth is named. You are not the god of confusion. Many men and women, mothers and dads, and children are confused about family dynamics as men and women are becoming lovers of themselves. We who are called by Your name, who belong to the family of God, put on the whole armor of God and take our stand against the prince of the air, the spirit who now works in the sons of disobedience.

Lord, we ask You to redeem families with the blood of Jesus, deliver them from the dominion of darkness, and translate them into the kingdom of light. We pray that mothers and dads will become vessels of love and understanding to their children; we ask for the restoration of broken, fragmented families.

Thank You, Father, for causing families to abide in a peaceful habitation, in secure dwellings, and in quiet resting places so they will lead their families out of the wellspring of wholeness.

SCRIPTURE REFERENCES: *Psalm 68:5-6; 2 Timothy 3:1-4; Ephesians 2:1-3*

Note

1. Pastor Irvin Whittaker, Christ the Victor Christian Center.

PRAYERS
OF
REPENTENCE

*Repent therefore and be converted, that your sins may
be blotted out, so that times of refreshing may come
from the presence of the Lord, and that He may send
Jesus Christ, who was preached to you before, whom
heaven must receive until the times of restoration
of all things, which God has spoken by the mouth
of all His holy prophets since the world began.*
—Acts 3:19-21 NKJV

REPENTING FOR THE EVILS COMMITTED IN THE UNITED STATES

We first read about the repentance of a nation in the Old Testament book of Jonah. When the people heard Jonah's message, they believed and turned from their evil ways. There are conditions to national restoration. Two things are necessary. First, we must repent! Unfortunately, the church of America has adapted the teachings of Jesus to political correctness and allowed the absolutes of the Bible to be replaced by the New Morality. May God forgive us! True repentance is a decision that results in a change of mind, which in turn leads to a change of purpose and action. Repentance requires me to renounce my old way of life and submit my life to the control of the Holy Spirit. Second, we must be converted and turn from our evil ways. Conversation is not magic; it is not a one-time experience but an ongoing transformation as the mind is renewed by the Word of God. This results in an about-face.

There is a law of sowing and reaping. Today, we are reaping the consequences of legalized abortion and same-sex marriage. But, it is not too late for America! In every generation God has sought for a man who would stand in the gap and build a hedge, to turn away His wrath from mankind (see Ezek. 22:30). Will you commit to take your position in the Body of Christ, stand in the gap, and build up a hedge for this generation? God has reconciled us to Himself and given to us the ministry of reconciliation.

PRAYERS OF REPENTANCE

Returning to my First Love

Most Holy Father, I left my first love, and remember from where I have fallen. I replaced my sweet fellowship with You with good works. I repent for devising my own plans and making ministry about me. The more my responsibilities increased the more I turned to self-improvement and trying to please others. Now, here in the quietness of this moment I remember with great longing those years of sweet fellowship when You spoke to me through the pages of the Bible.

With the help of the Holy Spirit I am returning to You and purpose to do the first works. As a deer gets thirsty for streams of water, I truly am thirsty for You, my God. I am here to ask only one thing, LORD: let me live in Your house every day of my life to see how wonderful You are and to pray in Your temple. I see the LORD All-Powerful, and I cry out with the heavenly host, "Holy, holy, holy, LORD All-Powerful! The earth is filled with Your glory!" It's all about You, LORD! It's all about You!

SCRIPTURE REFERENCES: *Revelation 2:4-5; Psalm 42:1-2 CEV; Psalm 27:4 CEV, Isaiah 6:1-5 CEV*

Personal Prayer of Repentance for a Ministry Leader

Father, even though I held fast to Your name and did not deny Your power, as the ministry grew, I devised my own plans and became concerned with how to maintain and promote growth of my ministry and congregation. Nothing is hidden from You, and I thank You for remaining faithful even when I wasn't. Today, I'm coming back to You and seeking first Your Kingdom and Your way of being right and doing right as a ministry of the Gospel.

I repent for manipulating the Gospel to fit with today's culture. I have sinned by compromising the truth of the Gospel and seeking the praise of men. Forgive me, O God, and cleanse me from all unrighteousness. I have sinned by courting the applause of men rather than speaking the truth in love. I submit to You, my Father, and turn from evil. I'm here to ask You to forgive me for leading others astray. According to Your Word as a ministry leader, I will be judged more strictly than others, and I'm asking You to lift this heavy load of condemnation. Forgive me for seeing and condemning the sin in the lives of others while easily overlooking my own sins and shortcomings. Lead me to remove the plank from my eye so that I can lovingly help others experience the freedom of forgiveness. With overwhelming humility, I thank You for calling me to the ministry, and I make this commitment before You now—I purpose to be a good example to those who are under my influence. Humbly, I ask for more grace that I will have the boldness to train Christ's followers in skilled servant work until we're all moving rhythmically and easily with each other, efficient and graceful in response to God's Son, fully mature adults, fully developed within and without, fully alive like Christ. Not only will Christ's followers serve in the church, but they will be salt and light in the marketplace. I pray for them to do all things without complaining and disputing, that together we may become blameless and harmless children of God without fault in the midst of a crooked and perverse generation, among whom we are to shine as lights in the world, holding fast to the Word of life so that I may rejoice in the day of Christ that I have not run in vain or labored in vain. Forgive me for elevating American nationalism above the kingdom of heaven. Your kingdom come, Your will be done on earth as it is in heaven. I am in this world for such a time as this, but I am not of this world. I am returning to my first love, Jesus, and purpose to magnify the name of Jesus so that all will be drawn to You, fulfilling the Great Commission. This I pray in the powerful name of Jesus.

SCRIPTURE REFERENCE: *Revelation 2:12-17; Ephesians 4 MSG; Matthew 6; Philippians 2:14-16 NKJV*

Prayer of Repentance for Intercessors

Father, raise up a company of worshipers in America who will seek Your face and help us to orchestrate together with a network of intercessors who can move in the power of unified prayer. Father, we were so excited to discover that we had power over the enemy forces, and we tried to take a stand against the forces of darkness before we were prepared. Rather than waiting for the Holy Spirit to lead us, we rushed to take a stand against the demonic forces before we learned who we were and how to walk worthy before You and with one another. Forgive us for being puffed up and misusing the gifts of the Spirit. Forgive us for insisting that everyone agree with our opinions and, even in the light of truth, holding fast to having it our way. Father, proving that we were right became more important than being right, and our prayers were no longer offered with pure motives. We confess that we prayed prayers of witchcraft over our leaders, even attempting to deliver them from demons when we were in error. Forgive us—we were wrong when we included gossip in our prayer requests. Forgive us for fighting against flesh and blood. We repent and turn away from idolatry—the works of the flesh. Today, we submit to You and resist the devil, knowing that he has to flee. O Father, give us the grace to renew our minds so we may hold the thoughts and purposes of Your heart toward sin and the cause of sin. When we pray for others, let it be from a heart of love for others. Help us to believe the best and pray for others with thanksgiving. May we be quick to listen to what the Spirit is saying and forgive others that we may not be exploited by Satan (for we are not ignorant of his schemes). Forgive our sins and cleanse us thoroughly by the blood of Jesus Christ so we can corporately pray prayers that will avail much at this critical hour in our nation, in the name of Jesus.

Prayer of Repentance for the Body of Christ

Father, we stand before You with bowed head, ashamed of not defending Your Church against the devil's tricks. We humble ourselves and confess that we allowed our minds to be diverted by the schemes of the enemy, justified blaming others for our failures, and we have sinned against You with our words spoken contrary to Your will. Forgive us for taking up the offense of past sins and blaming our ungodly attitude of unforgiveness on those who have wronged us. We will stand before You at the day of judgment and give an account for our personal deeds. Vengeance is Yours, and You will repay. Forgive us for agreeing with the enemy, holding others to a higher standard than we hold ourselves. Forgive us for voting for government officials who redefined family, gender, and marriage even though you instructed Your people to "Let marriage be held in honor among all, and let the marriage bed be undefiled, for God will judge the sexually immoral and adulterous" (Heb. 13:4). Forgive us for becoming lovers of money rather than being content with what we have. You have said, "I will never leave you nor forsake you" (Heb. 13:5). Therefore, we ask You to help us change the beliefs we have harbored and been taught from generation to generation, and renew our minds to Your Word. Then we will know how to do everything that is good and pleasing to You. Father, in the Scriptures You say, "I swear by my very life that everyone will kneel down and praise my name!" (Rom. 14:11 CEV). And so, each of us must give an account to God for what we do. Forgive us and help us to stop grumbling, complaining, and judging others. It's by grace that we also make up our minds not to upset anyone's faith, but we will be helpers of one another's joy. This we pray in the name of Jesus Christ, our Lord!

SCRIPTURE REFERENCES: *Ephesians 6; Hebrews 12; Romans 14*

Repenting for Pursuing the Acceptance of Man

Father, forgive me for allowing philosophies of man and the opinions of others to be exalted above truth, creating a division in the Church of Jesus Christ. A house divided against itself cannot stand, and I ask forgiveness for allowing theological arguments to separate me from my brothers and sisters who are called by Your name.

Show me how to make room for others, and help me to listen to those who have views different from mine. May I always listen to understand. Give me discernment so I will have eyes to see that our love for one another and core beliefs rule out arguments about our political and social differences. Jesus prayed that we would become one heart and mind, and acknowledge "Our Father, who is in heaven" (Matt. 6:9 AMP). Thank You that I live in a country where I can vote for those who will serve in positions of authority in our city, state, and nation. Forgive me when I do not get to know the people who will serve as my representatives. Give me discernment to know how to vote. I purpose to pursue peace with all people and holiness, without which no one will see the Lord. I choose to look carefully lest I fall short of the grace of God, lest any root of bitterness springs up top cause trouble, and by this many become defiled. Forgive me when my actions betray what I say, when I vote in elections contrary to Your Word. May I never settle for less than radical obedience to You, the Giver of life.

As I have opportunity, let me do good to all, especially to those who are of the household of faith, in the name of Jesus.

SCRIPTURE REFERENCES: *John 17; Hebrews 12:14-15; Galatians 6:9-11*

Repenting for the Division in the Church

Our Father in heaven, holy is Your name. We pray for Your will to be done on earth even as it is in heaven. John saw a great multitude from every nation, tribe, people, and language (see Rev. 7:9). Father, I ask You to forgive us, the people who are called by Your name, for tolerating prejudice toward one another. We raise up the banner of love and take our stand against the accuser, the father of lies who uses racism and the pain of the past to separate us from unity. We are a people whose identity is in Christ, and by the power of the Holy Spirit we will walk together clothed in the armor of God. We declare that we are strong in the Lord and the power of His might. Taking unto ourselves the whole armor of God, we are able to stand against the schemes of the devil and declare that we are one—red and yellow, black and white—we are one!

In the name of Jesus I bind my mind, will, attitudes, and emotions to the blood of Jesus, the control of the Holy Spirit, and the love of God. With the authority of Jesus, I loose, smash, and cast down every argument and every high thing that exalts itself against the knowledge of God. I bring every thought into captivity to the obedience of Christ.

Father, thank You that the truth makes us free from the influence of public opinion. The Holy Spirit has come upon us and lives in us enabling us to live out our glorious, Christ-originated faith. Father, forgive us for segregating ourselves by color, by a measure of wealth or intellect. We are one blood, redeemed by the blood of the Lamb who was slain before the foundation of the world. We are brand-new creations, baptized into Christ, and we have put on the family likeness of Christ. We rise and call for an end to division and segregation in our family—no division between Jew and Gentile, slave and free, male and female, white and black. Among us we are all equal—we are all in a common relationship with Jesus Christ. The kingdom of faith is now our home country, and we are no longer strangers or outsiders. We belong here, raised up together, seated in heavenly places in Christ Jesus far above prejudice and every name that would divide us, in the name of Jesus.

SCRIPTURE REFERENCES: *Ephesians 6:10; Ephesians 2*

Prayer of Repentance on Behalf of America

Lord God of heaven, O great and awesome God, You who keep Your covenant and mercy with those who love You and observe Your commandments, please let Your ear be attentive and Your eyes open that You may hear the prayer of Your servant, which I pray before You now, day and night, for the children of Israel, Your servants, and confess the sins of the children of America who have sinned against You. Both my father's house and I have sinned. We have acted very corruptly against You. We cast our votes in governmental elections for leaders who walk and lead our nation toward deeds of unrighteousness—we opened the doors of our nation for the rise of satanic practices, legalized the killing and mutilation of our unborn, and redefined marriage and gender identification. You created us male and female, and now our government and courts are doing away with who You created us to be. Forgive the sins of our forefathers who broke treaties with the Native American Indians and forced them to leave their ancestral homelands. Forgive our leaders from years past who believed in buying and selling people created in the image of God. We have not kept the commandments, the statutes, nor the ordinances that love compels us to obey. O Lord, I pray, please let Your ear be attentive to the prayer of Your sons and daughters who revere Your name. We ask You to forgive us.

This is how much You loved the world—You gave Your Son, Your one and only Son, so that no one need be destroyed. Lord, come and heal our land in the name of Jesus.

Prayer of Repentance[2]

Father, in the name of Jesus we come with humble and contrite hearts to repent of our sins against You and the Body of Christ. We come with one heart, one mind, and in one accord to disarm and take away any legal right the enemy may have over Your people and our country, the United States of America. We have walked in pride, having haughty spirits and attitudes, thinking that we have no reason to repent. We ask You to forgive us for engaging in friendly fire, attacking our brothers and sisters, shooting our own wounded because we may not agree with them. We repent of our arrogance, for murdering others with our words. We repent for having a religious, legalistic, and critical spirit, creating chaos, aiding the kingdom of darkness, and committing spiritual treason by dividing the brethren. Father, in the name of Jesus we repent for not operating in a spirit of unity, for not loving one another and extending to them mercy and grace. We ask You to heal the division that has separated us and give us the strength, maturity, and the discernment to push away everything that is separating us from You and from one another. May we operate as the one true army You have chosen us to be. We repent for not taking our stand against the forces of darkness by the authority that is in the name of Jesus. We seek Your face, asking for a release of Your power, the delegated authority to do the things You have called us to do in these end times. Dear God, we pray that the spirit of deception and lying will become unacceptable to Americans again. Forgive us for winking at sin, which has invited more deception. May we no longer be hardened to sin. God, forgive us—we have sinned. Lord, send another spiritual awakening and rescue us from our destruction, in the name of Jesus! Then I am reminded that where sin abounds, grace does much more abound!

Thank You for hearing our prayer of repentance, forgiving us, and restoring to us the joy of our salvation. We will be laborers of the harvest going into all the world making disciples of all nations. Amen and so be it in the name of Jesus.

Notes

1. This is based on a prayer written by David L. Thomas in *From the Heart of an Intercessor*, (Anderson Publishing: Douglasville, Georgia).

2. Prayer based on Mark Taylor, "Prayer of Repentance," September 7, 2017, http://www.sordrescue.com/uploads/4/7/7/9/47798703/prayer_of_repentance.pdf.

SECTION IV

INTERCESSORS
IN ACTION

by Pastor James (Jim) Tippin

Intercede means simply to pray for, to appeal on behalf of others. While in training, we will maintain focus on scriptural prayers. Intercessory prayer takes place in the throne room. Read Ezekiel 22:30-31 and Hebrews 4:16.

Pastor Tippin, a board member of Word Ministries, Inc., writes prayers for our Facebook friends and is the moderator of our Tuesday night prayer conference call. Whether you are a seasoned prayer warrior or new to intercessory prayer, I encourage you to pray and meditate on these prayers. Go to our website www.prayers.org for more information on how you can unite with us in prayer.

—Germaine

93

Day 1

Heavenly Father, thank You for the government leaders of America who are not ashamed to kneel and pray together in public. We saw congressmen united in prayer after a horrific shooting in our nation's capital. Our help comes from the Lord, and we enter into agreement with men and women who are unashamedly praying for one another in the public arena. Today, we pray: Our Father in heaven, hallowed be Your name. Your Kingdom come, Your will be done in America and all the nations even as it is in heaven (see Matt. 6:9-10).

Day 2

We cry out; hear our cry, O God, listen to our prayer; from the end of the earth we call to You when our hearts are faint. Lead us to the rock that is higher than we are, for You have been our refuge, a strong tower against the enemy (see Ps. 61:1-3). Hear our cry for America; hear our cry for America! Holy Spirit, give us the intercession of Jesus for our nation that we might release the sounds of united prayer on earth even as it is in heaven.

Day 3

Heavenly Father, many are standing on the spiritual wall, watching and praying for America. Unite us as a nation, unite us as a people, unite believers in our land. We are one Body, overcomers by the blood of the Lamb and the word of our testimony. Hear our cry; hear our prayer. In Jesus' name, amen (see Rev. 12:11).

Day 4

Heavenly Father, we are watchmen on the wall offering our prayer with thanksgiving as we intercede for America to be one nation under God with our many unique cultures and profound heritages of families. Thank You, Father, for the divine protection given. In Jesus' name, hear the voice of our pleas for mercy when we cry to You for help, when we lift up our hands toward Your most holy sanctuary (see Ps. 28:2).

Day 5

Abba Father, show the American people how to forgive ourselves and one another. I ask You to give us the grace to let go of all bitterness, wrath, anger, clamor, slander, and malice. Show us how to demonstrate to one another in our conversations and actions the decision to forgive, in Jesus' name (see Ephesians 4:31-32).

Day 6

Father God, here in Your throne room we entrust the future of America into Your keeping. We know that we can trust You and that You are able to safely guard all that we entrust to You until the return of Christ Jesus. It is in the name of Jesus Christ we thank You for hearing the cry of Your sons and daughters for America. We wait patiently for the Lord; You incline to us and hear our cry (see Ps. 40:1; 2 Tim. 1:12).

Day 7

Abba Father, America has known Your love, Your grace, and Your mercy. We reverenced You at one time, and we are praying that America will have another spiritual revolution. We thank You for the many miracles that You have performed by the name of Your Son, Jesus. You are the same yesterday, today, and forever. You have restored Your truths again and again in response to the prayers of Your children. We read about the spiritual awakenings, and we are here once again to offer our prayers of intercession with thanksgiving for our nation. We pray that America will turn back to You and once again reverence You. May we be salt and light to the nations. Hear our prayer, O Lord; let our cry come to You (see Ps. 102:1).

Day 8

Heavenly Father, I pray today for the President of the United Sates, his family, the Vice-President, his family, and all those serving our nation. First of all, I come before You to make petitions, prayers, intercessions, and prayers of thanks for all people, for rulers, and for everyone who has authority over us. I pray for these people "so that we can have a quiet and peaceful life always lived in a godly and reverent way" (1 Tim. 2:2 GW).

Day 9

Abba Father, we are Your people and the sheep of Your pasture giving You glory and praise for America, a nation founded on Judeo-Christian principles. You are our Creator, and we pray that the privilege and freedom to pursue You shall continue without governmental interference. The Bible is our standard of conduct. Often we have strayed, fallen short; forgive us and hear the cry of Your people this day. Apply Your grace and mercy to us, to this land once again. In Jesus' name, "with my whole heart I cry; answer me, O Lord! I will keep Your statutes" (see Ps. 119:145).

Day 10

Fellow intercessors, it is important not to manipulate or use Scripture in an attempt to control God. Manipulation is a form of witchcraft, a work of the flesh. Worship God and adore Him. Confess any sin that would hinder your prayers, knowing He is faithful to forgive and cleanse you of all unrighteousness. Offer prayers of thanksgiving and supplication. Listen to the Holy Spirit as you pray; He will give you the Father's heart.

> *The one who searches our hearts knows what the Spirit has in mind. The Spirit intercedes for God's people the way God wants him to* (Romans 8:27 GW).

Day 11

Lord of the Harvest, we ask You to send out workers into the harvest fields (see Matt. 9:38). We know it is Your will that all be saved and come to the knowledge of the truth. Thank You, Holy Spirit, for convicting men, women, boys, and girls of sin and showing them their need for salvation; give them knowledge of who Jesus is that they might know Him and the power of His resurrection.

Day 12

Every day is Thanksgiving Day for the believer. Let us pause and reflect on the blessings we enjoy as a nation. Regardless of today's date, we are reminded to be grateful that our government set aside a special day of Thanksgiving Day, and we remember to offer a prayer for our friends, the Native Americans, who shared their food with the Pilgrims. Pray with me:

> Father, we thank You for all Native Americans. You placed eternity in their hearts. Heavenly Father, we ask You to pour out Your blessings on our brothers and sisters of every tribe of the Native Americans. We consider this: "The heavens are yours. The earth is also yours. You made the world and everything in it" (Ps. 89:11 GW). We're in good hands!

Day 13

Praying is a privilege, and setting aside a specific time for meeting with Father-God is important. Stop and consider this—you are called to Mount Zion, to the city of the living God, the heavenly Jerusalem, and to the gathering of countless happy angels; and to the church, composed of all those registered in heaven; and to God who is Judge of all; and to the spirits of the redeemed in heaven, already made perfect; and to Jesus Himself, who has brought us His wonderful new agreement; and to the sprinkled blood, which graciously forgives instead of crying out for vengeance as the blood of Abel did (see Heb. 12:22-24). Take time to focus on the presence of the Lord. I like early morning before work. It may be only ten or fifteen minutes that you meet with the Father, Son, and Holy Spirit. Yes, there is an awesome task ahead for intercessors, but remember you are not alone. We are a global company of intercessors, united in the Spirit by an awesome God. It's all according to His plan. You are of great value.

> *I went to the Lord for help. He answered me and rescued me from all my fears* (Psalm 34:4 GW).

Day 14

Assignments from the Lord are before us. I've learned that there are short-term and long-term prayer assignments. Germaine shared about seeing two teenagers who were stopped by the police, and she was moved to pray for them. After just a few minutes, the prompting lifted. Long-term assignments are usually family, your local church, the city, state, and/or nation. One believer's long-term assignments included the nation of Israel; another cried out every day, "Lord give us China!" Whatever the assignment is, we use the Bible as our resource and manual for participating in prayer. Be faithful in prayer and to your assignment. Read Jeremiah 1.

Day 15

In the Old Testament, Daniel was praying and not receiving answers. Finally, an angel appeared to Daniel, saying to him his prayers were heard from the first day, but the answer was hindered due to a battle taking place in the heavenlies. Don't ever quit praying for America. There is a spiritual war taking place for the heart of the United States. When we pray according to the will of God, our prayers will be fruitful. Maintain your position in prayer! Read Daniel 9 and 10.

Day 16

Thoughts come to all of us—temptations to doubt and wonder if our prayers are doing any good. "Do I really matter? Is my prayer going to make a difference?" *Yes*, you are important—you matter! It takes each person doing their part to make up the whole. We are one Body! Oh, by the way, our God knows you by name. Keep praying for our nation, never give up, never give in, and refuse to grow weary in well-doing! The Bible assures us that in due season we will reap! Read Galatians 6.

Day 17

On the day of Pentecost, there were 120 in the upper room, and they were in one accord when *"Suddenly, there was a sound from heaven like the roaring of a mighty windstorm, and it filled the house where they were sitting"* (Acts 2:2 NLT). They were united in their obedience to Jesus who instructed them to wait for the promise of the Holy Spirit. You and I are following the direction of the Holy Spirit when we pray with all manner of prayers from all over these United States. Read Acts 1 and 2.

Day 18

Across our nation men and women are hearing the Holy Spirit. I was a teen when the Holy Spirit spoke to my heart about my life's work. Now that I am older I am seeing young and old alike praying for our nation. We learn the practice and discipline of prayer as we grow in grace and the knowledge of our God. The subject of prayer is inexhaustible. We are ever learning, ever growing, and ever achieving to the glory of our God! Let us pray for one another. "Be happy in your confidence, be patient in trouble, and pray continually" (Rom. 12:12 GW).

Day 19

When you pray, you are spending time with the Creator of the universe. Let that sink in; ponder this for a minute. How special it is—what a privilege to communicate with Someone who loves us unconditionally and is concerned with everything that concerns us. Stop and consider that for a few moments. Our God desires to reveal hidden secrets of His creation to us, and He moves in response to our prayers. He has included us in His plan for mankind. Think about it for another moment. We have an assignment to pray for our country!

> *First of all, I encourage you to make petitions, prayers, intercessions, and prayers of thanks for all people, for rulers, and for everyone who has authority over us. Pray for these people so that we can have a quiet and peaceful life always lived in a godly and reverent way* (1 Timothy 2:1-2 GW).

Day 20

Timetables, schedules, appointments, hurry up, and the list goes on. It took Moses 80 years to get where he needed to be to accomplish his destiny. He was in the desert when he saw the burning bush and had a conversation with God (prayer). He felt frustrated at times. We too can feel frustrated about how things look when we look around us and hear the news reports. Choose to set your mind on this: Our God prevails in all time, space, and circumstances. Consider the sparrow. "Don't be afraid! You are worth more than many sparrows" (Matthew 10:31 GW).

Day 21

Consider these words of Jesus: When the lights go out, no fanfare or applause is given; that is when the pray-ers will be needed most. Enter your prayer closet, obtain your instructions from Holy Spirit, and *pray*. All of heaven sees and backs you when you pray to the Father in the name of Jesus. We do not need to be seen by men for our worth to count. Jesus gave us instruction:

> *When you pray, don't be like hypocrites. They like to stand in synagogues and on street corners to pray so that everyone can see them. I can guarantee this truth: That will be their only reward* (Matthew 6:5 GW).

Day 22

As one called to pray for others, we remember "first of all."
First of all, we are to pray for all men, for the leaders of our
nation. Today we pray for the governors of each state. A
prayer we can pray together:

Heavenly Father, in response to Your leading we
intercede for the governors of each state in the
United States of America. We pray that they will
seek You for wisdom from above. We make an
appeal to heaven for the leadership of our nation
in the name of Jesus.

*If you are wise and understand God's ways,
prove it by living an honorable life, doing
good works with the humility that comes
from wisdom* (James 3:13 NLT).

Day 23

Pause and consider that you are seated in heavenly places together with Christ Jesus "far above any ruler or authority or power or leader or anything else—not only in this world but also in the world to come" (Eph. 1:21 NLT). Let's lift our voices as one voice:

Heavenly Father, we are here to intercede for the governors of the 50 states in the United States of America. Your wisdom and understanding will always make our nation great; may each governor acknowledge You in all their actions and words.

The [reverent] fear of the Lord [that is, worshiping Him and regarding Him as truly awesome] is the beginning and the preeminent part of knowledge [its starting point and its essence]; but arrogant fools despise [skillful and godly] wisdom and instruction and self-discipline (Proverbs 1:7 AMP).

Day 24

Let us pause and ask the Holy Spirit to help us avoid becoming entangled in the events of the day. We purpose to focus on Jesus, the Author and Finisher of our faith, as once again we prepare to pray for government leaders.

Heavenly Father, we pray for those who are elected to serve in the highest political office in the nation, not only in Washington D.C. but also in each state and around the globe. As they travel, may each one attend to Your words and treasure them. This I pray in Jesus' name.

My son, if you will receive my words and treasure my commandments within you, so that your ear is attentive to [skillful and godly] wisdom, and apply your heart to understanding [seeking it conscientiously and striving for it eagerly] (Proverbs 2:1-2 AMP).

Day 25

Today, we pray for military leaders. We always thank God, the Father of our Lord Jesus Christ, when we pray for the military leaders because we have heard of their faith in Christ Jesus (see Col. 1:3). We unite in prayer:

Heavenly Father, I intercede for the military leaders of our nation, the United States of America. I pray they seek You for wisdom from above and make an appeal to heaven for the leadership of our nation. If any lack wisdom in a circumstance, Holy Spirit, remind him to ask of God, who gives to everyone generously and without rebuke or blame, and it will be given him (see James 1:5).

Day 26

Consider this—the Word declares that you are strong in the Lord and the power of His might. Put on the whole armor of God that you may stand and withstand all the fiery darts of the enemy (see Eph. 6:10-12). Let us pray:

Heavenly Father, we pray that each of our military leaders and those under their command will serve the nation honorably and with sincerity. Keep everyone safe as they fulfill their responsibilities in service with the highest level of integrity. May their families feel and comprehend the love and respect due each one; may each one attend to Your words and treasure them. This I pray in Jesus' name.

Day 27

Allow these words to sink in; meditate on them as you prepare to take your place as a watchman on the wall:

> I thank my God upon every remembrance of the President, his cabinet, and all who are serving in our government. Always in every prayer of mine I make my request with joy. I ask for the salvation of anyone who may not be saved, and I pray that You will strengthen those who stand for righteousness. May Your will be done in America even as it is in heaven. Father, when You begin a good work, You perform it until the day of Jesus Christ (see Phil. 1-6).

Day 28

Today, we pray for the ministry leaders:

Heavenly Father, we pray for the men and women serving You, who are proclaiming the Gospel of Jesus Christ, each of the five-fold ministers in the United States of America and around the world. It is Your wisdom and understanding that will always make our nation great; may each five-fold minister acknowledge You in all their actions and words. May they reverently fear the Lord, worship and regard You as truly awesome, who is the beginning and the preeminent part of knowledge (see Prov. 1:7 AMP; Eph. 4:11-16).

Day 29

Father God, I remember that You bless those who bless Israel. We pray for the peace of Jerusalem and offer our prayers of supplication with thanksgiving. First, we pray for the Prime Minister of Israel and the other government leaders and the military. Give insight to danger and courage as each one stands guard against terror, and give them the strategy to overcome their enemies. I stand with the intercessors today asking for Your grace upon the Prime Minister of Israel and the people of this nation. Lord, may they abide under the shadow of the Almighty, in Jesus' name (see Psalm 91 and 122).

Day 30

Heavenly Father, we continue our intercession on behalf of the executives and managers of all media outlets in our nation—the cable networks, TV networks, radio, social media, print media, and the Internet of our nation, the United States of America. May Your wisdom and understanding always make our nation thrive, may each venue of the media acknowledge You in all of their actions and words.

The [reverent] fear of the Lord [that is, worshiping Him and regarding Him as truly awesome] is the beginning and the preeminent part of knowledge [its starting point and its essence]; but arrogant fools despise [skillful and godly] wisdom and instruction and self-discipline (Proverbs 1:7 AMP).

Day 31

Heavenly Father, our news is filled with attacks on cities around the world by terrorists; we see the carnage of human life; our planet is experiencing the consequence of sin. Yet according to Your Word, where sin abounds, grace much more abounds. May Your grace be recognized by the men and women in this day, may repentance be exercised in our cities and countries, may You grant us all Your mercy and grace. In Jesus' name (see Rom. 5).

—PASTOR JAMES TIPPIN, MSW
BA, Religious Education
Board Member of Word Ministries, Inc.
Retired Program Manager
Department of Human Services
State of Michigan

PREPARE FOR A
SPIRITUAL AWAKENING

Will there be another spiritual awakening in America? A sadness settles around with the news of earthquakes, floods, wildfires, riots on college campuses and in our cities, protests, hatred, and tragedies. Taking my place as a watchman on the wall, slowly these words appear.

> *The storms, the rioting, the shootings, and the constant propagandizing by the media are not who America is. America is red and yellow,*

black and white hands reaching out to the hurting and the dying. America is people coming together, helping one another to rebuild. I have prepared a people for such a time as this. Through many miracles I have preserved this nation for My purposes. The Constitution of America will stand, and America will survive because My people who are called by My name are praying.

The idea of nations originated with Me and I instituted government. My plan for nations began before the world began—before Christopher Columbus discovered America. I have trees that produce fruit for the healing of the nations.

Knowing that the Holy Spirit and the Word agree, I turn to the Scriptures for confirmation.

And he made from one man every nation of mankind to live on all the face of the earth, having determined allotted periods and the boundaries of their dwelling place, that they should seek God, and perhaps feel their way toward him and find him. Yet he is actually not far from each one of us, for "In him we live and move and have our being" (Acts 17:26-28).

Will there be another spiritual awakening in America?

Do not be deceived! America has been on a downward slope for many years through both Democratic and Republican administrations. My first direct encounter was when a public-school teacher requested prayer for our educational system. She had just learned that she was to teach her young students "situational ethics" rather than the absolutes of the Ten Commandments. America's values and our constitutional foundation was in jeopardy. The plans and devices of Luciferian forces were moving into our educational system to capture the hearts and minds of our children. They are becoming bolder in their efforts to overthrow the plan of God and remove God from our country. Our country and the Body of Christ is experiencing the "great divide," and a house divided against itself cannot stand. Our world is turned upside down. We look on in dismay as we hear good called evil, evil called good. Society as we had known it is spinning out of control.

America is in trouble, and some believe that this nation will not survive. The way back is filled with roadblocks and our political culture is in crisis mode.

As Christians we pray, and refuse to violate God's Word by voting for political candidates who are in favor of outlawing references to God, prayer from public places, and religious symbols. May God have mercy on us. We must be aware of the signs of the times.

> *Now, brothers, concerning the coming of our Lord Jesus Christ, and concerning our gathering together unto Him, we ask you not to let your mind be quickly shaken or be troubled, neither in spirit nor by word, nor by letter coming as though from us, as if the day of Christ is already here. Do not let anyone deceive you in any way. For that Day will not come unless a falling away comes first, and the man of sin is revealed, the son of destruction, who opposes and exalts himself above all that is called God or is worshipped, so that he sits as God in the temple of God, showing himself as God* (2 Thessalonians 2:1-4 MEV).

The America unfolding today is not the America of my youth. Each morning in our public schools we stood next to our desks and pledged allegiance to our flag. As I shared in the "Introduction," our teachers read a scripture and we prayed. We honored God and sang: *America, America, God shed His grace on thee, and crown thy good with brotherhood from sea to shining sea.* We were taught the history of our nation, knew our national anthem, and were thankful that we lived in the land of the free and the home of the brave. Many believed that America was "the hope of the world." During times of war and disasters, citizens came together and prayed for our President, for our military, their families, and our nation. In wartime our mothers volunteered at the Red Cross and our fathers who were exempt from war served in their communities. Although we did not all vote alike, we respected one another and held the same values. We desired freedom, not just for America but for the world. We believed "wherever the Spirit of the Lord is, there is freedom" (2 Cor. 3:17 NLT). Unfortunately, the church has exchanged the knowledge of God for political correctness, softening her views on sin and the consequences of sin (Rom. 6:23).

The turning point may have been in 1962 when prayer was removed from school. A spiritual, political, economic, and cultural revolution was in progress. The unseen forces behind the government will continue their destruction of America until "there arises in the Church believing groups who shall *agree* that this state of affairs shall no longer continue. And as such bands, with one accord, exercise a spiritual will of freedom for these lands, saying in the name of the Lord, 'This shall not be!' the unseen dominant forces shall be dominant no longer but shall yield ground, and the barriers shall fall."[1] I invite you to come with me and many others who are on this prayer adventure. It is the time to bow our knees before the God and Father of our Lord Jesus Christ, pray, and seek His face on behalf of America! "If Americans know who they are, and where they really come from, they will exert themselves even more to surpass previous generations. That is why the study of our history remains of critical importance. Our history is not just the story of who we once were, but of our destiny; not of what we have accomplished, but of our future success."[2] Are you expecting the works of God to be displayed in our nation, so all nations will know that He is God and there is none above Him?

We are in the middle of something miraculous. The Church is awakening from her slumber! Satan's tactics have been exposed to the light—the forces of evil are no longer working undercover. Clothed in the armor of God, we stand without wavering, working while it is still day for the night is coming. There is a divine destiny to be fulfilled! God is moving and America will be saved if God's people who are called by His name will seek first His righteousness and walk in the light of His Word. Darkness cannot comprehend or overtake the light! Grasp and take hold of the precious and exceeding great promises. Jesus said, "Have faith in me when I say that the Father is one with me and that I am one with the Father. Or else have faith in me simply because of the things I do. I tell you for certain that if you have faith in me, you will do the same things that I am doing. You will do even greater things, now that I am going back to the Father. Ask me, and I will do whatever you ask. This way the Son will bring honor to the Father" (John 14:11-13 CEV). The day of the "greater things" is here. The prayers of the righteous shall avail much if we meet the conditions of the New Covenant to love one another as Jesus loved us (John 13:34-35)

Just like all mankind, the founding fathers of this nation were not perfect. "They shared well-defined convictions concerning religious principles, political precepts, fundamentals, and long-range social goals."[3] They were men of good character and honor, who believed all men are created equal. One of their major arguments was about slavery. "An honest review of America's past would note, among other observations, that the same Founders who owned slaves instituted numerous ways—political and intellectual—to ensure that slavery could not survive."[4] The Holy Spirit guided them as they formed a government of checks and balances where citizens are free to vote for their government officials who would be responsible to them. The Christians of that day were "salt and light." The spiritual leaders called sin, sin and preached holy living. They believed that all men are created equal, and the Constitution was written to "share power with those who had none, whether they were citizens of territories, former slaves, or disenfranchised women."[5] We are a government of the people, by the people, and for the people.

People need to be aware that they are assenting and signaling agreement when they vote for political candidates and parties that support policies and programs that run counter to God's laws. Your vote does count and is a vote for life or for death! We have a responsibility to vote for life that we and our children might live.

God Prepares His People for the Last Days

The people who are called by the name of God have been raised together with Christ where we are seated far above "principalities, and power, and might, and dominion, and every name that is named, not only in this age but also in that which is to come" (Eph. 1:21 MEV). God Himself had an eternal view when He introduced us into this sphere. The accuser of the brethren will attempt to stop us, but if we are living a life of holiness in the presence of God, we learn to overcome him by the blood of the Lamb and the word of our testimony (see Rev. 12:11). "The blood represents not only the cleansing from the guilt and power of sin, but it is also the witness of that overwhelming victory gained at Calvary by virtue of which the Lord is now seated on high."[6] We are here for such a time as this.

1. God has made His people brand-new creations, partakers of His divine nature, and He gave to us the ministry of reconciliation. Believers are His representatives here on planet earth, and the Holy Spirit is our Counselor. "And all of this is a gift from God, who brought us back to himself through Christ. And God has given us this task of reconciling people to him" (2 Cor. 5:18 NLT). Let's imitate our Father, be true ambassadors who are strong in the Lord and the power of His might, speaking the truth in love.

2. Jesus, gives us the keys to the kingdom of heaven! The gates of hell cannot prevail against the Church united! How we use the keys we have been given determines our influence for good or evil. Keys are for opening and closing. When God raised Jesus from the dead and seated Him at His right hand, His Body (the Church) was raised from the dead and seated there

together with Him. We are seated with Him far above principalities, powers, dominion, and every name that is named not only in this world but in the world to come. May the Holy Spirit open the eyes of our understanding and bring us together! These terms, *bind* and *loose*, are legal terms that release the supernatural power of God to intervene in the affairs of life.

3. Jesus gives believers authority over the enemy! Jesus said, "Look, I have given you authority over all the power of the enemy" (Luke 10:19 NLT). The apostle Paul prayed that believers would know "the exceeding greatness of His power toward us who believe, according to the working of His mighty power which He worked in Christ when He raised Him from the dead and seated Him at His right hand in the heavenly places, far above all principality and power and might and dominion, and every name that is named, not only in this age but

also in that which is to come. And He put all things under His feet, and gave Him to be head over all things to the church, which is His body, the fullness of Him who fills all in all" (Eph. 1:19-23 NKJV).

4. God gave us His armor. "Finally, my brethren, be strong in the Lord and in the power of His might. Put on the whole armor of God, that you may be able to stand against the wiles of the devil. For we do not wrestle against flesh and blood, but against principalities, against powers, against the rulers of the darkness of this age, against spiritual hosts of wickedness in the heavenly places" (Eph. 6:10-12 NKJV).

God has not changed! He is the same today, yesterday, and forever. The Church has the keys to the kingdom of heaven. Jesus said, "On this rock I will build my church, and death itself will not have any power over it. I will give you the keys to the kingdom of heaven, and God in heaven will allow whatever you allow on earth. But he will not allow anything that you don't allow" (Matt. 16:18-19

CEV). Church, we have exceeding and precious promises. Let's unite and hold fast to the promises of God! By the grace given to us and the keys we hold to the kingdom of heaven, America shall be saved!

Praying for the Spiritual Awakening

The rapidly approaching end of the age is witnessing a tremendous increase in the activity of the powers of darkness. Unrest among the nations, more intense than at any previous time in earth's history, is due largely to the stirring up of the ambitions and passions of men, while the spread of an almost wholly secularized education is quietly doing away with the scriptural standards which formerly exerted a restraining influence among the so-called Christian peoples. Godlessness, which we have condemned so strongly in the Soviet Union, is almost equally as pronounced, though less blatant, in our own land.[7]

Are you praying for America out of your relationship with a Father who desires that all men be saved and come to the knowledge of the truth? God is love, and His love has been imparted to us by the Holy Spirit. It is time for the Church to pray, realizing that faith works by love. Jesus prayed for us.

> *I do not pray for these alone, but also for those who will believe in Me through their word; that they all may be one, as You, Father, are in Me, and I in You; that they also may be one in Us, that the world may believe that You sent Me. And the glory which You gave Me I have given them, that they may be one just as We are one: I in them, and You in Me; that they may be made perfect in one, and that the world may know that You have sent Me, and have loved them as You have loved Me* (John 17:20-23 NKJV).

Let us honor one another so our prayers for a spiritual awakening in America will not be hindered.

Always be humble and gentle. Patiently put up with each other and love each other. Try your best to let God's Spirit keep your hearts united. Do this by living at peace. All of you are part of the same body. There is only one Spirit of God, just as you were given one hope when you were chosen to be God's people. We have only one Lord, one faith, and one baptism. There is one God who is the Father of all people. Not only is God above all others, but he works by using all of us, and he lives in all of us (Ephesians 4:2-6 CEV).

Prayer is spiritual business, and the conditions for answered prayer for our nation are clear.

If my people who are called by my name humble themselves, and pray and seek my face and turn from their wicked ways, then I will hear from heaven and will forgive their sin and heal their land (2 Chronicles 7:14).

God moves in response to the prayers of His people. The miracle has begun, and it is my prayer that together we will move with the Spirit of God and offer up prayers that avail much!

Government has been ordained by God to "protect innocent human life and liberty, establish and enforce justice, and defend a nation from foreign and domestic threats."[8] The Church has the responsibility of praying for everyone.

> *Ask God to help and bless them all, and tell God how thankful you are for each of them. Pray for kings and others in power, so that we may live quiet and peaceful lives as we worship and honor God. This kind of prayer is good, and it pleases God our Savior. God wants everyone to be saved and to know the whole truth* (1 Timothy 2:1-4 CEV).

It is time for serious spiritual warfare inside and outside the prayer closet! The book of Ephesians is a prayer manual that gives insight on how to successfully stand against *all* the forces of darkness. Our prayers will avail much if we walk in love, walk in the light, and conduct ourselves like people with good sense. These are evil times, so we are to make every minute count. The writer of Ephesians gives a warning—do not take part in the unfruitful works of darkness rather than exposing them. It is written: "When anything is exposed by the light, it becomes visible.... Therefore it says, 'Awake, O sleeper, and arise from the dead, and Christ will shine on you'" (Eph. 5:13-14). My dear brothers and sisters, let us arise and go to the prayer room of heaven where Jesus is making intercession for the world.

The signs of the times are pointing toward the soon coming of Jesus, and we must be about our Father's business. The soul of our nation is hanging in the balance. The stakes are high! America has never known the division that we have in our country. God has given the Church a grace period, and while we have a president who is pro-Israel and pro-Christianity it is time that we seek the face of God, join in with the prayers of generations, and pray for the harvest of souls. At this present time, the Body of Christ is the agency here on earth that is restraining the evil one! (See 2 Thessalonians 2.)

Jesus, the Head of the Church, has defeated Satan, and we are children of the light radiating the victory He won on that resurrection morning. We are strong in the Lord and the power of His might. God has given us authority to reign in life, and the resurrection of Jesus empowers us to stand against all the forces of darkness. He raised us up to sit together in heavenly places *far above* all rule and authority and power and dominion.

Standing Against Unseen Forces of Darkness

We are in a spiritual battle for the soul of America. Let us not be tricked by the lying vanities of the New World Order; remember, we have the mind of Christ. I am thankful for believers who remain on guard, who are willing to do the research and keep us informed on how the enemy is sneaking around trying to destroy the works of God.

> *For those who know the value, and understand the potency, power, might, and worth of prayer, let us continue to pray ever fervently for our increasingly divided nation. As I have said many times before, friends, there are increasingly subversive, malevolent forces mightily at work, working feverishly to undermine*

the relatively "quiet and peaceable lives" we have been privileged to enjoy for so many years. Make no mistake here friends, the forces to which I refer are luciferian in nature, globalist in worldview, subversive in their approach, and chaotic in their tactics, looking to "agitate to the point of conflict" in order to enact the fundamental, wholesale changes in the US constitutional infrastructure (leading up to the desired "new international paradigm") which they so desperately seek.[9]

Unfortunately, many in the church have been asleep, even complacent and unaware that an insidious plot was quietly at work undermining the constitutional foundation of America and our Judeo-Christian values. We are in the middle of a culture war on every level! Our enemy is Satan whose plot is to take our thoughts captive and squeeze them into the modern day mold while he steals our children, kills Christianity and destroys the foundation of our nation. It was subtle in the beginning as a generation of college students was indoctrinated with anti-American, anti-Israel, anti-Christ, fear-filled propaganda.

"By starving the sensibility of our pupils we only make them easier prey to the propagandist when he comes."[10] The propagandists came and stayed!

The Church must wake up and pray according to the will of God for this country as never before. "We also have to train the next generation of Christians for what it will face as [the enemy] continue[s] advancing [his] agenda through whatever means possible."[11] Now is the time to lay aside our differences and recognize that we are in a fight to the finish. Let's hear the apostle Paul's message in the language of today:

> *And that about wraps it up. God is strong, and he wants you strong. So take everything the Master has set out for you, well-made weapons of the best materials. And put them to use so you will be able to stand up to everything the Devil throws your way. This is no afternoon athletic contest that we'll walk away from and forget about in a couple of hours. This is for keeps, a life-or-death fight to the finish against the Devil and all his angels. Be prepared. You're up against far more*

than you can handle on your own. Take all the help you can get, every weapon God has issued, so that when it's all over but the shouting you'll still be on your feet. Truth, righteousness, peace, faith, and salvation are more than words. Learn how to apply them. You'll need them throughout your life. God's Word is an indispensable weapon. In the same way, prayer is essential in this ongoing warfare. Pray hard and long. Pray for your brothers and sisters. Keep your eyes open. Keep each other's spirits up so that no one falls behind or drops out (Ephesians 6:10-18 MSG).

"If we will allow our minds to be renewed continually by the Word of God, we will spot immediately when we, or the world, have gone off course and need correction."[12] The Holy Spirit will show us what to pray and how to pray so our prayers will release heaven's intercession into the atmosphere. The sounds of heaven and earth will meet preparing the way for the "New Jerusalem, that holy city, coming down from God in heaven" (Rev. 21:2 CEV). Satan has been defeated, but he continues to lure mankind with the same temptations He used in Matthew 4. Let us do what Jesus did, and escape every temptations. Do not be naive; do not be deceived. We are in a crisis.

Let us choose to lay aside all that would hinder our prayers—anger, wrath, malice slander, unforgiveness, obscene talk, jealousy, and lying to one another. Spiritual warfare takes place in the prayer room and outside the prayer room. The weapons of warfare are not of the flesh, but they have divine power to destroy strongholds. Let us go forth with the weapons of warfare armed with compassion, kindness, humility, meekness, patience, forgiveness, and love (see Col. 3). When we are walking in the love of God—walking in the light—our prayers will avail much!

Before You Pray for America

Are you ready to pray for America and the end-time harvest? "Search me, O God, and know my heart" (Ps. 139:23). Before you pray, ask God to give you His heart and reveal His plans and purposes for this nation. Your faith works by love, so ask the Holy Spirit to help you overcome any negative, judgmental attitude toward anyone. We are here to pursue the plans and purposes that the will of God might be done in America and around the world even as it is in heaven. Be prepared to enter Spirit-led, Spirit-filled spiritual warfare. Spiritual warfare addresses Satan and his regime. God has been involved in the history of America from the beginning—performing miracles when there seemed to be no way. America is the largest nation to embrace Christianity. The founders of these United States of America acknowledged the King of Kings and Lord of Lords. John Dickinson, a signer of our Constitution, declared:

> *Kings or parliaments could not give the rights essential to happiness.... We claim them from a higher source—from the King of kings, and Lord of all the earth. They are not annexed to us by parchments and seals. They are created in us by the decrees of Providence which establish the laws of our nature. They are born with us; exist with us; and cannot be taken from us by any human power, without taking our lives.[13]*

We have a surer word from Jehovah, the King of Kings and the Lord of Lords.

We know that God is always at work for the good of everyone who loves him. They are the ones God has chosen for his purpose, and he has always known who his chosen ones would be. He had decided to let them become like his own Son, so that his Son would be the first of many children (Romans 8:28 CEV).

Notes

1. John A. MacMillan, *The Authority of the Believer* (Camp Hill, PA: WingSpread Publishers, 2007), 42.

2. Larry Schweikart and Michael Allen, *A Patriot's History of the United States: From Columbus's Great Discovery to America's Age of Entitlement* (New York: Sentinel, 2014), 867.

3. W. Cleon Skousen, *The Five Thousand Year Leap: a Miracle That Changed the World* (Salt Lake City, UT: Freemen Institute, 2013), 29.

4. Schweikart, *A Patriot's History of the United States*, xvi.

5. Ibid.

6. MacMillan, *The Authority of the Believer*, 34.

7. Ibid., xiii.

8. Joel C. Rosenberg, *Implosion* (Carol Stream, IL: Tyndale House Publishers, 2012), 324.

9. Pastor Irvin Wittaker II, Christ The Victor Christian Center, Wiggins, MS.

10. C.S. Lewis, *The Abolition of Man* (New York: HarperOne, 2008), 15.

11. Erwin W. Lutzer and Steve Miller, *The Cross in the Shadow of the Crescent* (Eugene, OR: Harvest House Publishers, 2013), 37.

12. David Jeremiah, *I Never Thought I'd See the Day!* (New York: FaithWords, 2011), xxi.

13. John Dickinson, "An Address to the Committee of Correspondence in Barbados (1766): Of the Right to Freedom: and of Traitors," qtd. in Edmund Clarence Stedman, ed., *A Library of American Literature: Literature of the Revolutionary Period, 1765 1787*, (1888), 176.

INTERCESSORS, YOU HOLD THE ANSWER! WILL AMERICA BE SAVED?

We hold these truths to be self-evident, that all men are created equal, that they are endowed by their Creator with certain unalienable Rights, that among these are Life, Liberty and the pursuit of Happiness. — That to secure these rights, Governments are instituted among Men, deriving their just powers from the consent of the governed, — That whenever any Form of Government becomes destructive of these ends, it is the Right of the People to alter or to abolish it, and to institute new Government, laying its foundation on such principles and organizing its powers in such form, as to them shall seem most likely to effect their Safety and Happiness.

A CALL TO ACTION: PRAYER, POLITICS, AND ACTIVISM

by Dr. Carol M. Swain

If my people who are called by my name humble themselves, and pray and seek my face and turn from their wicked ways, then I will hear from heaven and will forgive their sin and heal their land.

—2 Chronicles 7:14 ESV

America has reached the point where it is increasingly clear that politics and activism alone cannot rescue our nation from its steady decline toward sin and degradation. Nor can politics and activism restore our nation's Judeo-Christian heritage or enable us to use our resources and power effectively around the world. Politics and activism cannot cure what ails our nation.

What America needs is eloquently outlined in the prayers found in this book. In Second Corinthians 10:4, we are reminded, "The weapons of our warfare are not carnal, but mighty through God to the pulling down of strong holds" (KJV). America needs power that can only come from the effective integration of the weapons of spiritual warfare with practical tactics and strategies. In addition to targeted prayer and fasting, we need a new form of activism within religious and secular organizations. Christians of all ages need to answer a new clarion call to use their strategic placement to engage in regular prayer and fasting *within* their workplaces and educational settings. The goal is spiritual awakening and transformation using these spiritual weapons of warfare. A combination of prayer, politics, and policy changes can be initiated and led by Christians who are now employed in corporations, secular media organizations, colleges, and universities, as well as public and private schools.

Insider wisdom gleaned from those who understand the secular world can combine with spiritual knowledge to frame targeted prayers and strategies to combat the different forms of evil that invade and dominate certain spheres. Enhanced knowledge of institutions and workplaces can prepare one to pray more effectively for strategies and tactics to improve the environment and reach the lost. We should not lose sight of the fact that many non-believers are frustrated too, and they are unhappy with the direction of society. God can create opportunities for us to share the Gospel and enlist help even from those who might not agree with us on many issues. Our victory will come if we cooperate with God's positioning and plan for our lives. Only God can give us the strategies and power to fight in a manner that weakens, and in some cases destroys, the demonic strongholds exercising undue influence over our leaders and institutions. We battle with the knowledge that the ultimate victory will come from Christ's return and the establishment of His kingdom. In the meantime, we work to push back the darkness through spiritual revival and awakening that can bring many others to Christ before the doors of opportunity are closed.

To be effective in our quest, we must first get the attention of the people who profess to be Christians. Unfortunately, there are millions of Americans who identify themselves as Christians but repeatedly support causes and politicians who endorse programs and policies that run counter to biblical injunctions about righteousness. My first attempt to address this occurred in 2011, when my book *Be the People: A Call to Reclaim America's Faith and Promise*[1] was released. *Be the People* was an effort to educate, encourage, and exhort Christians to stand up and be the people who would fight to reclaim America's Judeo-Christian heritage. Sadly, a number of people who say they love the Lord give their allegiance to things His Word condemns.

But there is hope! We can take special solace in Second Chronicles 7:14, where God promises to heal and restore nations that position themselves to receive His intervention. If we want America restored, we must humble ourselves, acknowledge our collective sins, and ask Him for forgiveness.

We stand guilty, because under our system of government it is "We the People" who elect the politicians who enact their programs and policies on our behalf. Therefore, we bear responsibility for the evil we see in Washington and across America in our cities and towns.

Some years ago, theologian Vern Polythress stated that Christians have not achieved much change using politics because politics follows cultural trends rather than leads them. Polythress correctly observed that "a temporary victory in the voting booth does not reverse a downward moral trend driven by cultural gatekeepers in news media, entertainment, art, and education."[2] Syndicated columnist Cal Turner reached a similar conclusion: "Thirty years of trying to use government to stop abortion, preserve opposite-sex marriage, improve television and movie content and transform culture into the conservative Evangelical image has failed."[3]

Our ability to shift the culture toward righteousness has failed and it continues to fail because we are battling powerful institutions that include a corrupt government, a secular leftist media, morally compromised schools and universities that often teach hatred of America and intolerance toward orthodox Christians and Jews. As Steve Feazel and I show in our book *Abduction: How Liberalism Steals Our Children's Hearts and Minds,*[4] our children are targeted as young as kindergarten and they are exposed to efforts to strip them of their moral innocence. There is a blatant agenda to secularize them and remove positive influences gleaned from Christian homes. There is a concerted effort to strip our children of traditional morality and any recognition of absolute rights and wrongs and replace them with cultural relativism.

Like ancient Israel and Judah, we have engaged in a willful embrace of evil and a rejection of the holy, righteous God who holds people and nations in the palm of His hand. Many of our political and religious leaders call good evil and evil good. We should be concerned about God's judgment of our nation and whether He will continue to protect us and shield us from the evil intents of more wicked nations. We know from Malachi 3:6 that the Almighty God does not change His righteous standards. Isaiah 55:8-9 reminds us that His thoughts are not our thoughts and His ways are not our ways. God's thoughts are much higher than our thoughts and so are His standards. Throughout the Bible,

God promises blessings for obedience and curses for disobedience (see Deut. 28).

The future of America is in our hands—yours and mine. Will we be blessed or cursed as a people? We need not ponder these matters in ignorance. We know from the prophet Jeremiah that is possible for a nation to reach the point that God will no longer hear the intercessors' prayers: "Therefore do not pray for this people, nor lift up a cry or prayer for them; for I will not listen when they call to Me because of their disaster" (Jer. 11:14 NASB). We need faithful ones who can read the signs of our times. Watchmen on the wall who are willing to say, "Here I am! Send me" (Isa. 6:8). Those who pray without ceasing. Let us be those people!

Notes

1. Carol M. Swain, *Be the People: A Call to Reclaim America's Faith and Promise* (Nashville: Thomas Nelson Press, 2011).

2. Vern Polythress, qtd. in *Be the People,* 222.

3. Cal Turner, qtd. in *Be the People,* 222.

4. Steve Feazel and Carol Swain, *Abduction: How Liberalism Steals Our Children's Hearts and Minds.*

ABOUT GERMAINE COPELAND

Germaine Copeland is the author of the best-selling *Prayers That Avail Much* book series. Founder of Word Ministries, Germaine travels nationally and internationally conducting prayer schools, speaking at churches, conferences, and other groups. As she ministers, people are encouraged by her insights on praying effectively, experience emotional healing, and learn how prayer promotes personal change, making a measurable difference in the spiritual climates within their spheres of influence. Germaine and her husband, Everette, have four adult children, eleven grandchildren, and eleven great-grandchildren. They reside in Greensboro, Georgia.

RECOMMENDED READING

Be the People
by Carol M. Swain, PhD

*Abduction: How Liberalism Steals Our
Children's Hearts and Minds*
by Steve Feazel & Dr. Carol M. Swain, PhD

*A Patriot's History of the United States:
From Columbus's Great Discovery
to America's Age of Entitlement*
by Larry Schweikart and Patrick Allen

Prayers That Avail Much for the Workplace
by Germaine Copeland

*The 5000 Year Leap: A Miracle
that Changed the World*
by W. Cleon Skousen

The Light and The Glory
by Peter Marshall and David Manuel

FREE E-BOOKS?
YES, PLEASE!

Get **FREE** and deeply-discounted **Christian books** for your **e-reader** delivered to your inbox **every week!**

IT'S SIMPLE!

VISIT lovetoreadclub.com

SUBSCRIBE by entering your email address

RECEIVE free and discounted e-book offers and inspiring articles delivered to your inbox every week!

Unsubscribe at any time.

SUBSCRIBE NOW!

LOVE TO READ CLUB

visit **LOVETOREADCLUB.COM** ▶